**Previous titles by Darryl Vidal**

*Next Practices: An Executive Guide for Education Decision Makers*

*Vision: The First Critical Step in Developing a Strategy for Educational Technology*

*Confucius in the Technology Realm: A Philosophical Approach to Your School's Ed Tech Goals*

# Fail to Plan, Plan to Fail

## How to Create Your School's Education Technology Strategic Plan

Darryl Vidal

ROWMAN & LITTLEFIELD
Lanham • Boulder • New York • London

Published by Rowman & Littlefield
A wholly owned subsidiary of The Rowman & Littlefield Publishing Group, Inc.
4501 Forbes Boulevard, Suite 200, Lanham, Maryland 20706
www.rowman.com

Unit A, Whitacre Mews, 26-34 Stannary Street, London SE11 4AB

© 2017 by Darryl Vidal

*All rights reserved.* No part of this book may be reproduced in any form or by any electronic or mechanical means, including information storage and retrieval systems, without written permission from the publisher, except by a reviewer who may quote passages in a review.

British Library Cataloguing in Publication Information Available

**Library of Congress Cataloging-in-Publication Data Available**

ISBN 978-1-4758-3416-1 (cloth : alk. paper)
ISBN 978-1-4758-3417-8 (pbk. : alk. paper)
ISBN 978-1-4758-3418-5 (electronic)

∞™ The paper used in this publication meets the minimum requirements of American National Standard for Information Sciences—Permanence of Paper for Printed Library Materials, ANSI/NISO Z39.48-1992.

Printed in the United States of America

# Contents

| | |
|---|---|
| Introduction | ix |
|     Scope of this Book: MAPIT™ Planning | x |
|     What Is MAPIT™? | xi |
|     Why Is MAPIT™ Different? | xii |
|     Who Needs MAPIT™? | xiii |
|     When Is MAPIT™ Needed? | xiv |
|     How to Use MAPIT™? | xv |
|     What Are the Benefits of MAPIT™? | xv |
|     Who Initiates MAPIT™? | xvi |
|     How to Initiate MAPIT™? | xvii |
|     Executive Sponsorship | xviii |
|     MAPIT™ Planning Processes | xviii |
| **1**   Needs Identification | 1 |
|     The Discovery Process | 1 |
|     The Open Systems Interconnect Model | 3 |
|     Inputs | 4 |
|     Discovery | 5 |
|     Stated Board of Education Goals and Objectives | 6 |
|     Federal or State Mandated Planning or Compliance | 6 |
|     Interviews | 7 |
|     Kick-off Meeting | 7 |
|     The Interview Process | 8 |
|     Departmental Interviews | 9 |
|     Leadership Interviews | 10 |
|     Surveys | 11 |
|     Scoping of the Discovery Process | 11 |

| | | |
|---|---|---|
| | Compilation of Interview Data | 13 |
| | Gaining Buy-in | 14 |
| | Consensus | 15 |
| | Discussion | 16 |
| | Objections | 16 |
| | Background | 17 |
| | Existing Systems Configurations | 18 |
| | Relevant Systems | 19 |
| | Design Narrative | 21 |
| | Compilation | 21 |
| | Objectives | 22 |
| | Scope and Scale | 23 |
| | Scenario One—Wi-Fi Implementation | 23 |
| | Scenario Two—Student Information System (SIS) Selection | 24 |
| **2** | **Needs Analysis** | **25** |
| | Educational (Business) Needs | 26 |
| | Scenario One—Wi-Fi Implementation | 27 |
| | Scenario Two—Student Information System (SIS) Selection | 27 |
| | GAP Analysis | 28 |
| | Systems Needs | 29 |
| | Scenario One—Wi-Fi Implementation | 30 |
| | Scenario Two—Student Information System (SIS) Selection | 30 |
| | Systems Modification | 32 |
| | Systems Development | 32 |
| | Technical Needs | 33 |
| | Technology Infrastructure | 33 |
| | Technology Platforms | 34 |
| | Scenario One—Wi-Fi Implementation | 35 |
| | Scenario Two—Student Information System (SIS) Selection | 37 |
| **3** | **Recommendations** | **39** |
| | Planner Perspectives | 41 |
| | System Recommendations | 42 |
| | Design Direction | 43 |
| | Rough Order Magnitude Cost Modeling | 46 |
| | Scenario One—Wi-Fi Implementation | 47 |
| | Scenario Two—Student Information System (SIS) Selection | 52 |
| | Technical Recommendations | 54 |
| | Scenario One—Wi-Fi Implementation | 55 |
| | Scenario Two—Student Information System (SIS) Selection | 56 |
| | Preliminary Design | 58 |

| | | |
|---|---|---|
| **4** | **Feasibility Study** | 61 |
| | Budget Sources | 63 |
| | Funding Cycles | 64 |
| | Prioritization | 65 |
| | Phasing | 66 |
| | Final Recommendations | 67 |
| **5** | **Design and Implementation** | 69 |
| | The Strategic Plan | 69 |
| | System Design | 74 |
| | Logical Design(s) | 75 |
| | Design Narrative | 76 |
| | Physical Layouts | 77 |
| | Implementation Plan(s) and Timeline (GANTT Chart) | 78 |
| | ROM Budget Estimates—Cost Model | 79 |
| | Final Notes | 79 |

About the Author     81

# Introduction

More than 80 percent of technology projects fail! What does that mean? In planning and project management parlance, it means the project has broken one of the three constraints (aka Triple Constraint): scope, time, and budget. These three factors hold the key to a functional strategic plan and their subsequent implementation plans to define the successful Education Technology project.

The real-world outcome is always more painful than the innocuous triple constraint. This could mean the students' laptops don't connect to the Wi-Fi. Or they do, but they're slow. Or maybe the new Student Information System (SIS) doesn't support State Reporting requirements. Or maybe the Learning Management System isn't compatible with the Directory Services.

In the Education Technology planning and project management field, methods have been developed that help mitigate Ed Tech and IT project failures: strategic planning and project management. But typing "strategic planning" into a browser search will return more resources and training than anyone would ever need to run a small- to medium-sized Ed Tech or IT project. One might ask, if it's a small- to medium-sized project, then is a strategic plan even necessary?

The answer is a resounding YES! Because of the *technology* factor. The fact is that technology, and more specifically, education and information technology systems are inherently complex and must be analyzed, planned, prioritized, budgeted, justified, and approved. We're not talking about building a space shuttle here. We're talking about a $50,000–500,000 IT project that necessitates formal structured planning and project management. And without a structured approach, statistics show that over 80 percent of these projects will break the triple constraint—meaning that $50,000–$500,000 could be at risk, or at the very least, underperforming or over budget. In addition, think of the associated risk to the persons responsible for the project and the monies. Aren't they just as responsible and accountable to these failures?

The first important factor to be considered in all Education Technology endeavors is that all technology projects are inherently complex. More than just installing a software upgrade during lunch, or swapping out an edge switch. IT directors have learned this the hard way over the past decades.

Why? Because over the past three decades, schools and school districts have become 100 percent dependent on their Education Technology and IT systems. Yes—100 percent!

Imagine how a school district would perform transportation, cafeteria, and student attendance if any portion of the IT support systems were to come to a halt. What if a school district has a power outage and administration can't locate the students? Even a failed storage network fabric or software incompatibility could cause a catastrophic technology event, and these aren't even examples of complex projects.

One mantra that Education Technology planners and project managers should live by: Projects should not cause problems. This mantra can be used to keep the project planner two-to-three steps ahead in the game. The better the planner is at planning, the easier the project manager's job.

One of the major factors in Ed Tech and IT project failures is that IT professionals don't typically receive formal project management training. The balancing factor is that most project management training is not specific to Education Technology or IT. Since these methodologies are comprehensive and all encompassing, they become too complicated and impractical for the typical small-scale technology project.

To address this planning and project management scope issue, a methodology evolved called Management and Planning of IT (MAPIT™).

This is where the two phases connect: planning and managing.

This series of books, "Fail to Plan, Plan to Fail," is comprised of two books: *MAPIT™ Planning* and *MAPIT™ Project Management*. Throughout this book, references are made to the planner as the person in charge of developing the plan. Each step of the MAPIT™ Planning process will be mastered and documented by the planner. It will be contingent on the planner to understand the importance of each step, use each step to its fullest capacity to lay the groundwork for a successful project, and provide enough detail and specificity for the project manager to be successful. Remember, a successful plan can only be so if the project management is also successful.

## SCOPE OF THIS BOOK: MAPIT™ PLANNING

The scope of this book is the MAPIT™ Planning process. MAPIT™ Planning is patterned after industry-recognized strategic planning architectures but has been optimized for two specifics: Education Technology (including Information Technology) and "small-to-medium-sized" scale.

Now this category of small- to medium-sized differs according to the organization. A small-scale IT project might range from $20,000 to $500,000—anything more would be a large project. In the State and Local Government category, these IT projects might range from $25,000 all the way up to $2,000,000 and still not be considered a large project. In school districts, however, projects as large as $2,000,000 or up to $5,000,000 still aren't that large, when considering a large school district might have over one hundred sites and an IT modernization budget in the hundreds of millions. MAPIT™ Planning processes will support technology projects of this size and scale.

## WHAT IS MAPIT™?

MAPIT™ is a practical and effective planning and project management methodology designed specifically for Education Technology projects.

What makes technology projects different from building bridges and airplanes?

All Education Technology projects need planning and management. Even the smallest "project" can disable an entire enterprise. Think about the time the network engineer needed to update some switches and found a manufacturer's bug in the upgrade that took down the whole network. Or the time a new printer was to be installed that triggered a software upgrade that was incompatible with a production application rendering the department offline.

These types of occurrences can only be mitigated through planning and communication—both fundamental aspects of MAPIT™.

MAPIT™ was developed originally in 2000 to address the planning and management of complex IT projects. As the author researched the existing project management methods and certifications, it became markedly clear that these project management models were too big and unwieldy for small- to medium-sized IT projects. These traditional models and methods are intended to aid in the management of large-scale programs like constructing buildings and designing factory production lines.

Even relatively small technology projects can also be highly complex, leveraging new technologies, and requiring infrastructure and facilities to support their ongoing nature. As technology has become more and more a key to classroom capability, school operations, and automation, the successful deployment and implementation of technology projects become critical success factors for the school or district as a whole.

MAPIT™ as a set of methods and processes are scaled and customized for the technical project, leveraging the Open Systems Interconnection (OSI) model for analysis, and standard planning processes like Needs Analysis and Feasibility. But, by providing tools and methods specific to the technical aspects of Education Technology projects, MAPIT™ can and will provide the planning and support processes that can aid the technology project manager to plan, anticipate, communicate, and successfully deliver small- to medium-sized Education Technology projects.

## WHY IS MAPIT™ DIFFERENT?

The basic uniqueness of MAPIT™ is that it is scaled for small- to medium-sized technology projects, and yet it provides a basis for sound strategic planning and project controls. The processes are tightly scoped and based on constant client interaction. The planner must take each step as detailed in this book in order to provide the breadth and depth required to deliver a plan that can be managed to implementation success. The planner will be required to develop documentation at each phase. These will be used to review and revise with the client and stakeholders at the end of each process. This constant interaction, forces the planner to interact and gain credibility and validity of the plan from its earliest stages.

The processes of MAPIT™ are a series of self-contained processes that require inputs, actions, and provide outputs or deliverables that become inputs to the succeeding process. Each of the deliverables will be compiled to encompass a formal Strategic Technology Plan.

The deliverables are functional and actionable. Each process output becomes a documented chapter for the formal report. They either serve to support justification of the need, or they will become inputs for future requirements or specifications. In any matter, each process will produce important pieces to the Strategic Technology Plan deliverable.

The budgets are based on feasibility and the timelines are realistic. There is nothing worse than a consultant or planner who starts the process, then goes away and comes back with a plan that holds no basis with reality and hasn't been qualified by a legitimate feasibility study or a realistic timescale for completion. The MAPIT™ Planning processes are clear, concise, and will deliver clarity.

Figure 0.1 depicts the entirety of the MAPIT™ Planning and Project Management processes. This book pertains specifically to the top half of figure 0.1—the Planning process.

The MAPIT™ process has been used and refined repeatedly through the years and has also been written about extensively in previous books: *N3XT Practices: An Executive Guide of Education Decision Makers* and *VISION: The*

Introduction                                                                 xiii

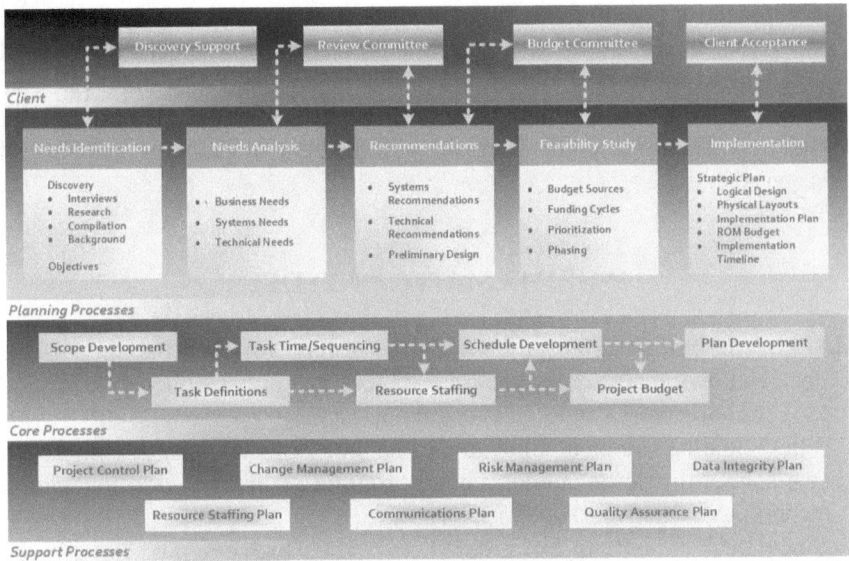

Figure 0.1   MAPIT™ Planning and Project Management Processes.

*First Critical Step in Developing a VISION for Education Technology*, both published by Rowman & Littlefield Education.

## Planner Perspectives

One of the key factors of successful technology planning and project management is the active role of the consultant or the planner. This text, as a descriptor of the practices and methods, will also inform the reader as to the perspective and attributes of the planner himself: How he must present and communicate his role, his scope of responsibility, and as well as how to manage and set expectations. At each phase and module of this text, an attempt will be made to provide planner perspectives and insight to the challenges and nuances experienced during the planning process.

## WHO NEEDS MAPIT™?

Any Education Technology professional can benefit from the use of MAPIT™ Planning and project management methods. If a school computer technician recognizes a training issue, then by meeting with the IT director and developing a training plan, the organization can benefit. If a network engineer communicates a potential downtime and the director stops the upgrade until all departments are informed, a possible disaster may have been diverted. If the systems administrator identifies a product incompatibility and does some research, a future problem may have been averted.

All these examples come from the enforcement of planning and project management.

## WHEN IS MAPIT™ NEEDED?

MAPIT™ is best used, any time a plan is needed for even the simplest IT project. Following are some specific instances that may be encountered:

- A new funding source or allocation of budget for technology systems, such as a school district technology bond program or district-wide foundation technology initiative.
- A new business initiative or production system, such as a new cloud-based SIS system.
- A new technology infrastructure project. A structured cabling installation or Wide-Area telecommunications service upgrade.
- A new school site or a new building.
- New leadership or administration.
- A major software upgrade required either for a server or client application. A desktop operating system upgrade.
- A hardware upgrade that may affect any production system. A server memory upgrade of a production system or a core switch redundant power supply replacement.

The problem with technology projects and the reason there are so many failures—defined at anytime one or more triple constraints are offended—is because technology projects are always more complex than they seem. Technology projects have inherent complexities. Here are some of the most salient reasons why:

- Technology projects have many interdependencies, such as power, hardware compatibilities, software compatibilities, driver updates, service pack updates, application updates, operating system updates, and backup and disaster recovery.
  - If all interdependencies are not considered in the planning of a technology project, it will be doomed to fail.
- Technology projects affect many different users. Not only their obvious users, but also external users, parents, suppliers, banking, and order processing.

- Any technology project that interrupts the business processes can become catastrophic.
- Technology projects oftentimes have hidden costs like software license upgrades, special software features, or overtime hours to complete a project. Even things such as patch cables and UPS systems can add tens of thousands of dollars to a project.
- Technology projects take longer than expected. Whenever the engineer says it will take an hour, plan on increments of eight hours. The engineer doesn't include planning, research, communications, validity checks, lab testing, and knowledge transfer when estimating the project duration.
- Technology projects are often misunderstood by leadership. Consider the cost of VoIP upgrades when the old analog handset would cost $35 and the new VoIP phone costs $250. Where's the cost–benefit?

## HOW TO USE MAPIT™?

First of all, MAPIT™ puts the brakes on any unplanned project without injecting significant delays. The planner or key stakeholder must know that from the beginning. If someone is going to say, "we need a plan" then that person better also be prepared to say, we need at least X number of weeks to develop the plan and it will cost $X to create this plan. If this delay and call for resources isn't backed-up by management, then the project will not stop, a formal plan will not be created—and someone is at risk of being part of the 84 percent of technology project failures.

One week of planning is worth four weeks of unplanned implementation—typically unplanned implementations are wrought with technical glitches, departmental delays, outages, and after-action reporting (what happened?). Remember the last time the network engineer said, "Don't worry, this will take 5 minutes. I'll do it during lunch."

These famous last words have seen school district networks crash and network cores fail due to software or BIOS incompatibilities. Urgency and criticality can always be measured by the number of users affected but what if a student's emergency contact can't be found, or the buses don't have their routes? Technology system upgrades, deployments, and migrations should always be looked at as mission critical—as if the school operations would be traumatically impacted.

## WHAT ARE THE BENEFITS OF MAPIT™?

The processes of MAPIT™ Planning are logical and thought provoking. If the planner follows each step, schedules each interaction, and produces each deliverable, then the processes will lead the planner and his project down a road of logical development, validation, technical alignment, feasibility, and detailed documents, budgets, and specifications.

Once all these processes are developed, documented, validated, and approved, there is NO CHANCE that this project will fail unless one of the underlying assumptions, validations, technical systems, funding sources, or leadership advocacy changes or if the project manager is unable to manage the plans within the triple constraints (that's the next book). That's one heck of a guarantee!

## WHO INITIATES MAPIT™?

This is always a great question. Who initiates a formal planning process? It is not necessary that the process be initiated by the superintendent of schools, but their unbending support is. If leadership even lets on a hint of skepticism, the entire process and the resulting plan is at risk.

In order to objectively identify how a formal planning process begins within a school or school district, there must be a trigger. An event that causes any ongoing concern to recognize the need to perform an evaluation and develop a plan.

This event can be a combination of any of the following events:

- New board of education initiatives or goals given
    - Whenever leadership has a planning or goal setting event, retreat, or off-site strategy session, it is commonplace for leadership at the highest levels as well as departmental levels to have some new edicts and goals to be achieved.
    - Once leadership acknowledges the need for a plan to support an initiative, therein lies the opportunity for someone to advocate for a formal planning process. One that needs to be organized and to involve all stakeholders—otherwise how will any of the objectives or changes be planned and implemented?
    - The biggest component to any failed endeavor is *informal* planning. The minute someone thinks, "that's easy, I'll just do it myself," or "we can do this in-house, let me handle it," and goes off and develops a plan in a vacuum without any stakeholder involvement; this is a recipe for project disaster.
- Annual or periodic review that heralds information requiring action, funding,—and—or resources
    - It is also very common for a minor irritant to explode into a major event. For example, a monthly review of a minor project delay, repeated too many times will become a major incident once leadership gets annoyed.

Once again, this is the time to say, "we need to fix this once and for all. We need to initiate a strategic technology planning process. We need to get everyone involved, and we need to plan and implement a solution that will address this issue. It will take resources. It will cost money."
- New funding sources that allow new investment in technology systems
  - Schools and school districts, often find themselves receiving one-time or recurring funding sources. A school district may issue a bond amounting to several millions of dollars to improve facilities and infrastructure.
  - These types of events REQUIRE formal processes for planning and project management. We've repeatedly seen school districts spend money without real-world formal assessment and planning only to see their projects fail and taxpayer money wasted.
- A failure or technology catastrophe
  - Sometimes there is no funding, but a major outage or technology failure is the perfect impetus to initiate a formal plan. This is the time to go to leadership and say, "No more quick fixes, we need to do a Strategic Technology Plan. We have to do it right. We can't have this happen again."
  - The conversation usually continues this way, "we did it that way last time, we have to stop and take a look at the whole project and all the interdependencies. We need to dedicate resources ($) to the planning to avoid another failure."
- New leadership
  - If a new school or district leader doesn't initiate some sort of assessment, then this person's leadership skills are clearly lacking. The process of learning a job and the organization is an assessment. The more formal a process that the new leader embraces,
    - the more stakeholders will be involved,
    - the more clear the objectives can be communicated,
    - the more accurate the planning and estimation,
    - the more real-world the fiscal planning can be, and
    - the more successful the implementation will be.
- The point of this discussion is that any event or occurrence can be the trigger or impetus to initiate a strategic technology planning process, and there is one fundamental requirement—commitment and endorsement by leadership.

## HOW TO INITIATE MAPIT™?

Any type of strategic planning must be formal. If it is not understood and recognized as a formal process, then it will be very easy at all levels of the organization to ignore or to not cooperate with the planning process.

Some of the most destructive early comments and attitudes that WILL be encountered when initiating a strategic technology planning project will be like the following:

- Who is this consultant? He doesn't know anything about our school district.
- Why are we doing this again? Nothing happened last time.
- Just give him what he asks for and nothing more.

## EXECUTIVE SPONSORSHIP

Executive Sponsorship is always and will always be the key to successful planning. If the leadership doesn't fully engage and agree with the objectives, the outcomes will be irrelevant. Although the superintendent may not fully engage in all meetings and all processes, initial advocacy and support at the highest level will be necessary for the planner to be successful and engender cooperation from the department leaders and staff.

## MAPIT™ PLANNING PROCESSES

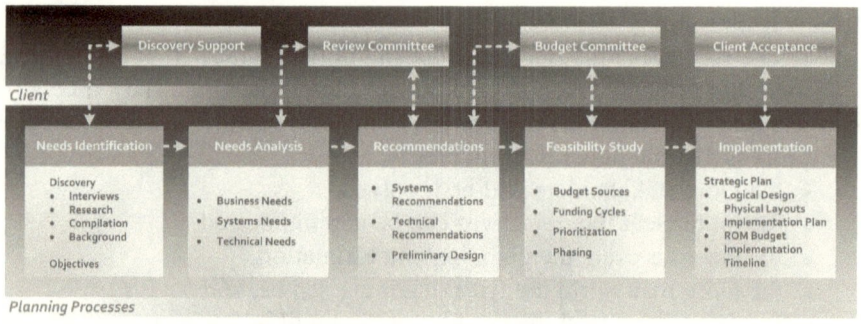

Figure 0.2  MAPIT™ Planning Processes.

## Chapter One

# Needs Identification

Needs Identification is the first stage of any planning methodology although nomenclature may differ (figure 1.1). One of the main challenges many Information Technology (IT) managers face is the lack of time and opportunity to follow a complete planning process, including an appropriately exhaustive Needs Identification process as detailed here. Throughout the execution of the methodology, many of the tasks and activities of each phase have a multilayered agenda. The first is obvious and the second, less so. The obvious agenda is to follow the process, take the client through the process, involve the client in every step of the process, obtain acceptance or acknowledgment of the results and deliverables at each stage, and deliver the plan on schedule so implementation can move forward. In addition, throughout this process the planner should be developing a trusted rapport with the client and stakeholders as well as develop credibility for the process.

The underlying agenda is always to attend to the needs of each stakeholder, add value to their respective scopes and needs during the process, support and validate their successful processes, and always act on behalf of their benefit and the organization's greater good. The planner should never be the star of the project or report, merely the messenger. By low-lighting the personality of the planner, the planner can emphasize the process and methodology.

### THE DISCOVERY PROCESS

Oftentimes, the stakeholders don't have a complete vision for how technology can impact their scopes of influence. In this way, the planner can provide insight into relevant research and best practices of similar industries and

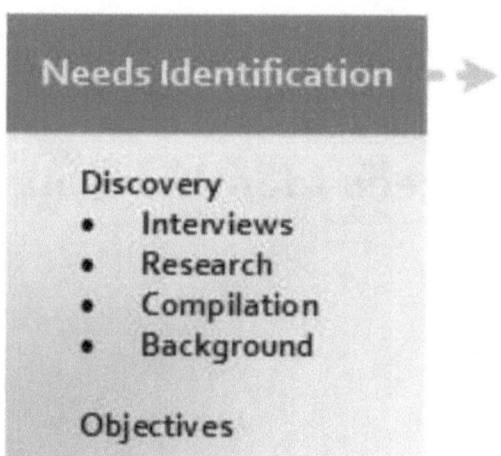

Figure 1.1  Needs Identification Process.

organizations. But only with significant background in these trends and practices can the planner lead these visionary discussions.

The focus of this early phase is on identifying "needs" as opposed to solutions. The planner must resist the urge to discuss the following during the discovery phase: solutions, technologies, architectures, manufacturers, and platforms. To do so is not only premature and likely misinformed, but it also short-circuits the methodology. The scope of the Needs Identification process is to develop objectives that address the needs identified during this process. These objectives will then be stated and tested in a review with the program stakeholders. As can be seen, the process is to engage with leadership and stakeholders at every phase along the way, in order to present the current direction of the plan, hear objections early on, and resolve or absolve them before continuing to the next step. If the planner negligently moves forward without some level of validation or acknowledgment to an objection, he risks developing the rest of the plan under a cloud of skepticism.

Oftentimes, the objectives may need to be restated so that the objection is mitigated in this early stage. For instance, if early in the interview process, it is clear that one leader wants iPads while another leader wants Chromebooks, the planner's job is to ensure that the objectives stated don't limit or bias the report to either platform. The objectives may state that the program supports both platforms (or all platforms), or the leadership may dictate that one platform is the standard, in which case the objector must simply accept the edict. At least in this case, this objection has been cleared early and by leadership and the planner can continue on to finalize the Needs Identification phase by developing the Discovery document, which includes the Inputs, Interview

Notes, Research and Background (logical designs—existing), and the project objectives.

The next phase—Needs Analysis—will utilize a systematic approach to understand first how the objectives translate into their granular components, Business Needs, System Needs, and Technical Needs. Again, the solutions planning or development is not happening at this stage. The planner must keep his and his clients' minds clear of these early deducements or proclamations. It is not until the Recommendations phase that the focus will move on to strategies and solutions that address the needs.

Of course that doesn't mean that the planner doesn't already know what the solution(s) will be. In any technology project, infrastructure will be required to support the networking of the technologies, whether they be wired or wireless. So if an organization's IT infrastructure is not up to the industry standard, then it would be very easy for the planner to jump to the recommendation portion of the process (for this scope and objective) and know inherently that new structured cabling and wireless networking equipment would be recommended. *But*, he better not make any assumptions because it isn't until after the Recommendations phase that the feasibility study will provide the real answers to what can and will be within the scope and scale of the plan.

The salient point of the Needs Identification process is to identify valid and acceptable strategic objectives, state them clearly and unequivocally, and present this phase and its output (Discovery document and Objectives) to leadership and stakeholders in order to move on to the Needs Analysis phase.

## THE OPEN SYSTEMS INTERCONNECT MODEL

The Open Systems Interconnect (OSI) Model, a seven-layered model for defining communications standards and protocols, has been defined by the International Standards Organization (ISO). This is one of the defining factors of technology systems that separates technology projects from more common projects such as construction or facility upgrades (figure 1.2).

The model can be used to provide a structured approach to technology Needs Identification by starting at the bottom and moving up.

This means in a typical MAPIT™ Needs Identification process, the planner would start at the physical layer and seek source documents and diagrams that inform about technology facilities and structured cabling. By moving up the model, the planner would then assess, in order: network equipment, network services, computing systems, and up-through applications. Keeping in mind that the OSI model provides guidelines and protocols for communications standards, the model can be successfully leveraged for all technology planning projects.

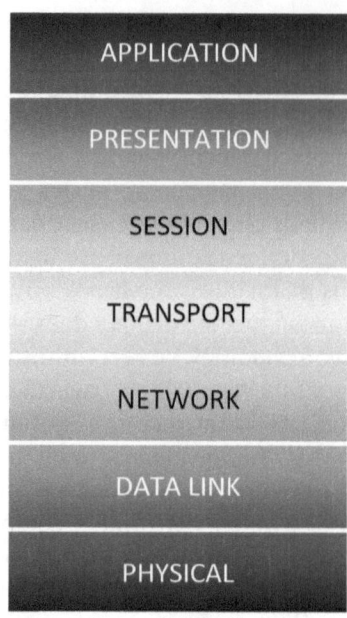

Figure 1.2  Open Systems Interconnect Model.

## INPUTS

Inputs are all the sources of data brought forward for each phase of the planning process. Each phase receives a set of inputs and delivers a set of outputs or results that then become the inputs of the next phase of the planning. For technology Needs Identification, these original source inputs might come from an organizational strategy plan or stated goals and objectives. If a Board of Education developed long-range goals, or Local Control Accountability Plans (LCAP), the recommendations within these reports could be relevant input sources.

Keep in mind, strategic needs must be reviewed and developed based on Education and Information Technology scopes. For instance, if the strategic plan is to increase graduation levels by a certain percentage, then the relevant technology scope might be to increase the use of learning management systems in an effort to make delivery more efficient and increase student performance to curricular standards. In the educational environment, Board of Education goals and objectives typically include flavors of student achievement, professional development of staff, parental and community involvement, and safety and security.

These types of enterprises and organizational strategic plans become the primary original source of inputs. The planner's role in Needs Identification is to redefine and rewrite the strategic objectives with a focus on technical capability of the enterprise.

## Planner Perspectives

At this early stage of Needs Identification, it is important that the planner avoids thinking about solutions, making recommendations, or offering quick responses to complex questions.

One saying that should be considered for every project planner is: "Questions are free, answers cost money."

At this point in the process, only questions are being asked, no answers provided. And the clients can ask as many questions as they like, but answers will be complete, researched, estimated, and well thought out, not shot from the hip during the early stages and not likely delivered until after the feasibility study.

## DISCOVERY

Similar to the legal discovery process, the MAPIT™ Discovery process is all about finding things out, and documenting them. This second part is significant and important enough to emphasize—if an informal written narrative and logical diagram of the existing systems and network is not developed, the most important details and analysis will be lacking. The act of creating the outline, organizing, and formalizing the notes into sentences and graphical diagrams will force the planner to research the systems and services and understand them to the point relevant to the scope. This level of attention to detail is what usually gets left out in the informal planning process, where the planner assumes many things and makes analysis and decisions based on incomplete background and information.

The more complete the background documentation during the Needs Identification process, the more researched and credible the outputs (objectives) should be. Not only the process of developing and compiling the information, but also the active review of these early documents by stakeholders will aid to keep all background and logical diagrams true to the environment.

There is nothing worse than getting near the end of a final report to find out that some of the early findings are wrong. What if someone left out the fact that the copper horizontal cabling is Category 5 instead of Category 5e, causing the planner to exclude the need for 10 Gbps-capable copper cable. The whole strategic plan and cost model would be completely out-of-whack.

Similarly, if the planner left out the complex detail about VMware Enterprise licensing, he might miss the $50,000 impact of this software licensing requirement.

## STATED BOARD OF EDUCATION GOALS AND OBJECTIVES

These leadership entities typically develop and publish strategic goals and objectives. By using these types of published reports or plans, the planner can immediately engage leadership by "wrapping himself in the flag," or appropriating the board goals.

If through this process, someone in leadership comments that the goals and objectives are obsolete or inaccurate, the effort has been established! Suddenly the planner has the opportunity to force these issues to the top and either advise them to allow the planner to help with the development of new business strategy, or at least work with leadership to define goals and objectives related to technology strategy.

Keep in mind that the planner will be using the MAPIT™ Needs Analysis process to develop the Strategic Technology Plan based on these objectives, so the planner cannot allow the leadership to take over or delay the planning process.

Gaining access to some of these documents may be sensitive. Especially if they're outdated. Be thoughtful when requesting these types of documents because they are the domain of executives and leadership, and even though they are there to guide them, they can also be points of accountability that they may be sensitive to.

## FEDERAL OR STATE MANDATED PLANNING OR COMPLIANCE

In education, Common Core State Standards are the obvious example of Federal and State Standards that must be considered in strategic planning.

By seeking and including all these factors as inputs for the MAPIT™ planning process, the planner can be seen as identifying truly strategic information to drive planning. These activities should be seen by leadership and stakeholders to reinforce the fact that the process is grounded in reality. If they don't feel that this accomplishes that, then there is obviously a problem with these plans.

These sources of input data should be collected and reviewed by the project client at the very early stage in order to challenge and validate the significance of each of the inputs.

In addition, asking these type of strategic questions will require leadership and stakeholders to take ownership of certain scopes. For instance, if a specific reporting requirement is part of the project scope, and a particular department head must facilitate communications to the government entity, then it will be in that department head's best interest to engage and support the planner. If he doesn't, he will be seen as an obstructionist by the other stakeholders. If planning moves forward without the support of key stakeholders with scoped responsibilities, the whole planning project is at risk of failure.

There is nothing worse than getting through a formal planning process and in the formal presentation, some high-level stakeholders say something that invalidates the whole plan. For this to happen, either the planner neglected to engage all key stakeholders, or one of these stakeholders purposely withheld information key to the project.

## INTERVIEWS

The formal discovery process includes a series of interviews with the key players and stakeholders beginning with the kick-off meeting.

It must be stressed that there is more than one objective to the interview process than data collection. The interview process will provide the planner the opportunity to:

- provide background of the MAPIT™ planning processes to gain their understanding and support by fostering credibility of the process and the planner,
- express, without proposing solutions, insight and understanding to their challenges and issues, again in order to lend credibility to the process and the planner,
- allow stakeholders to hear the thoughts and concerns of their peers in a structured, objective-oriented forum,
- set expectations of the timelines and deliverables, and
- support brainstorming of ideas from all staff to advocate an open communication.

## KICK-OFF MEETING

One of the most important objectives of the kick-off meeting is to get all the highest level stakeholders at the meeting. If the highest level leadership is not engaged and an advocate of the planning process, then the executive sponsorship component will be lacking, meaning that the plan can easily be tossed to the side if deemed invaluable by someone not at the kick-off meeting.

During the kick-off meeting, it will be important to have a clear agenda and cover the following items:

- Schedule of planning process
- Review of deliverables
- Schedule of departmental interviews
- Requests for documents and data
  - Due dates for these items
- Communications plan including:
  - Communications distribution list and key contact information
  - Weekly or standing status meetings
  - Reports and frequency.

## THE INTERVIEW PROCESS

As stated before, the interview process has multiple objectives. One of them is to build credibility of the process. By beginning the interview meeting with a review of the MAPIT™ planning process, the group will begin to understand the steps of the process and understand that they will have the opportunity to be a part of the process.

It is always a good idea to begin the meeting with introductions. Invariably, one or several will have more to say than just their name and title. This will give the planner the opportunity to watch the group dynamics and identify specific personality traits that may help and/or hinder the discovery process. Although the planner must take control of the meeting and keep it on task and on time, it is also important to hear out individuals who clearly have an opinion. Or at a minimum, take a note to revisit the issue later in the meeting, or after the meeting. Using phrases like, "excellent comments, we'll revisit that topic later," and "we'll be sure to discuss that topic before we leave this meeting," will allow the planner to keep the meeting moving without cutting off and bypassing important comments.

It is extremely important at this stage of the planning process to be totally inclusive and open to comments and suggestions. These meetings are key to ensuring that all voices are heard and understood. That doesn't necessarily mean that their input or suggestions will have any impact on the final plan. To balance this, the planner should also be in visual contact with the client in order to be cognizant about outliers—a person or persons set on disrupting the meeting or making negative comments.

If people come away from the meeting feeling that the process is credible and their input was noted and discussed, this is an enormous accomplishment for the planner. This must be done systematically and thoroughly. The planner

**Table 1.1 Sample Agenda**

| Agenda Item | Participants |
|---|---|
| Introductions | All, Sponsor |
| Review of Planning Process | Planner |
| Questions and Discussion Relevant to IT Project | All |
| Review of Salient Points | Planner |
| Requests: Tasks and Due Dates | Planner, All |
| Schedule | Planner |
| Adjournment | Planner |

should be sure to provide a clear outline or agenda for the meeting and keep to schedules. Finish the meeting by providing contact information for future communications and a quick review of next steps.

Action items should be discussed identifying key individuals and due dates. It is best to discuss these requirements in front of the whole group so that all those present are aware of the commitment (request) and due date.

If follow-up meetings with this group are planned, then these dates should be discussed and scheduled, at least tentatively, before the meeting is adjourned.

Table 1.1 is a sample agenda for Discovery Interviews.

## DEPARTMENTAL INTERVIEWS

The planner must systematically request to meet with each department relevant to the scope of the strategic planning. For instance, if the payroll system is specifically out of scope, the meeting with the payroll department for a wireless project is not necessarily warranted. However, if the HR department is requesting new tablet-based reporting, then they would be part of the interview process.

It is usually contingent on the planner to work with the key contact to determine these early scope definitions. It is always better to err on the side of inclusion than the opposite. The planner may see very quickly that the department is really on the fringe or out of the scope of the plan just by their comments and interest. If several members of the departmental interview process are clearly puzzled by the meeting, that is a pretty clear indication that their department is not impacted by the project scope. But the planner must recognize if they are correct in their interest or lack of.

For instance, in the example of the HR department requesting tablet-based reporting, the staff members may not be interested in the meeting itself, but the planner needs to understand their expectations from this "tablet-based reporting" capability. Maybe a manufacturer or software vendor has been showing them "smoke and mirrors" demonstrations that will not work in the actual environment. Or maybe what they want is not tablet-based at all.

**Planner Perspectives**

It becomes very important that the planner pays close attention of the time scheduled for these meetings. The planner must keep the meeting focused and finish on time. He must be able to query and note the discussions as well as who is making the comments. The more detail that can be noted during the meeting, the more information will be available to provide the background information of the Strategic Technology Plan that will result from this information. Also, for any items requested, record the party responsible and ask for a delivery date.

## LEADERSHIP INTERVIEWS

Interviews with leadership are the most important—for gaining and maintaining credibility, identifying objectives, and setting expectations. When meeting with executive leadership, these meetings should probably be near the end of the discovery process, after departmental meetings and dogged industry and technology research. This will allow the planner to have a fundamental understanding of the organizational dynamics, issues, trends, rumors, and suspicions.

Not to depict the planner as an insurgent or spy, but by meeting with departments and department heads, the planner will have interactions that the leadership lacks or is filtered from. This knowledge is as sensitive as it is valuable. By sharing tidbits of information with leadership, the planner can demonstrate a level of intimacy about the organization. However, this hand should never be overplayed. The planner should never insinuate that he knows more than, or things that, leadership is not aware of. This can be perceived as manipulative or insincere. The planner must always refer to the need for sound business principles, industry best practices, and IT process leadership.

**Planner Perspectives**

It is at these final discovery meetings that the planner should start to introduce possible objectives for the planning project. With the right stakeholders available, these meetings might end this way, "these are the two objectives I'm drafting for the objectives of this phase of the project. What do you think?"

Once again, by involving key players in the crafting of these objectives, they will feel included and invested in the plan.

## SURVEYS

In larger Strategic Technology Plans, surveys may be used to allow the planner to "touch" more people in a shorter amount of time. The survey can include both specific and open-ended questions that are specific to the project scope. Survey questions can even ask about specific technologies or solutions—even though they would be avoided in the discovery meetings—just to see what understanding, concerns, or biases may exist about these items.

Table 1.2 is a sample survey that translates quotes and themes from the survey and discussions and discusses and offers implications of these themes regarding technology strategy. By using this two-column format, comments that may be unclear or tangential can be focused by the planner by drawing inferences and implications of the comments.

Although there are many ways a survey can be used for the discovery process, the questions must be focused squarely on the scope of the planning. This can become an area out of scope and out of control. Also, if someone responds to the survey with strong comments, the planner is forced to address it in writing. Even in the example in table 1.2, many of the comments are incomplete or without context.

## SCOPING OF THE DISCOVERY PROCESS

Scoping of the Discovery and Background documents is extremely important. The difficulty of discovery becomes, "what is the scope of the discovery?" Meaning what all is going to be looked at? If the plan involves implementing a new accounting module that will affect everyone filling out timesheets in an organization, then all departments, with users of the time reporting systems, will be impacted and should be interviewed.

An example of clearly out of scope interaction might occur in a small-scoped accounting module upgrade process of a server running this accounting software. If all the equipment, software, and licenses are handled within the IT department, and the scope of the upgrade process involves only key departmental resources, then the discovery process may include only stakeholders within the IT department. That doesn't mean that the formal planning process should be abridged or informalized—quite the contrary. The more technical the stakeholders, the more critical their support and advocacy.

**Table 1.2  Sample Survey**

| Technology Committee Theme | Implications |
|---|---|
| "The first most important factor is authentic teaching and learning: this should precede any attempt to integrate technology." | Suggests that deploying technology with guidance or professional development that insures "authentic learning" is paramount. |
| "Hardware that can handle the requirements of the Technology Plan." | Suggests that hardware currently used by this teacher and others is not adequate for the intended or attempted application. |
| "Updated software in terms of Microsoft Suite and Adobe Acrobat." | Suggests a district standard for Office Suite and document handling. |
| "More focus on acceptable use." | Suggests that technology systems are being abused or used inappropriately. |
| "Classroom in 3 years? iPad, SmartBoard projector with speakers, Apple TV." | Restatement of current classroom standard. Reinforces need to implement in all classrooms. |
| "It would be wonderful to have technology (IT) support every single day on our site." | Suggests that technical support has not been available or responsive in the past. |
| "We need a site where teachers can find everything in one stop." | Suggests a content development and content management capability for sharing electronic resources. |
| "Three additional desktops per classroom to support students to accomplish tasks that cannot be done on iPads." | Suggests the need for student shared use computers for tasks that cannot be accomplished on district one-to-one platform. |
| "All books accessible digitally." | Seeking access to electronic resources including textbooks. |
| "Update all computers, two additional portable labs, 2–3 desktops in each classroom, wireless printing." | Suggests need for technology standards, lifecycle refresh, and print capability for mobile devices. |

To reinforce this concept, imagine this module upgrade being scheduled for the weekend to minimize production impact during the regular work week. Although all the departments that could be impacted should be notified in advance of the work, and informed of a downtime window, it is not likely that the accounting department head is a critical stakeholder for a software upgrade project.

But if the plan will clearly have organizational impact, then all departmental leaders must be presented an opportunity to be "involved." If the accounting department comes back on Monday to find their systems are down, this would be catastrophic. But if the department knew that there was a critical upgrade happening over the weekend, and there was a risk of an outage, then there would be fewer surprised and concerned users. That doesn't affect the urgency of the situation, but the communication in advance of the failure could mitigate a civil war in the trenches.

## COMPILATION OF INTERVIEW DATA

The compilation of interview data is a process of transcription of notes to a narrative document and the iterative feedback loop required to check and double-check the information developed. There is nothing worse than publishing a report with erroneous information in the very beginning of the report. This type of error could diminish—or worse, invalidate—the whole process in reality or in the eyes of the client organization.

There are many ways to present interview data. One common method is to list the date, time, and participants of the meetings, and then include topical discussion and supporting quotes. It is not necessary to credit quotes or statements to individual participants but the planner may elect to provide this data as it pertains to the report in relevance and scope.

A two-column table can be used to categorize comments into themes or areas of concern. By adding a column for the participants, the planner may elect to add names to statements or themes. It becomes of utmost importance to have follow-up conversations or communications to check validity and credit for specific or featured items or issues before publishing anything, even in draft.

The planner should not attempt to summarize or editorialize the meetings and their outcomes. It should be recognized simply as an informational document expressing relevant statements, concerns, objections, and objectives of the various stakeholders and interested parties. In fact, the more individuals and departments that can be engaged in the early planning process, the more engaged and impactful the study can become because the parties clearly participating and advocating become a cheering section within the organization. The planner may note that most people like to see their name in print. So, in general, it's better to include as many names as possible and then omit or remove them only if requested or corrected.

The planner should seek to engage, question, and follow-up with key players and stakeholders into the process as far as possible, while not allowing any individual to hijack or take control of the project.

It is common practice to label all discovery information as DRAFT until the absolute very final publication of documents, usually associated with a formal presentation or report review. The more departmental staff can review early drafts of the Discovery document, the more in-depth *relevant* data can be gathered.

**Planner Perspectives**

One of the main factors of strategic planning that the planner must understand and master is the fact that every interaction has at least two motives or agendas: first, to move the project forward; and second, to manage expectation of the client.

The first is obvious, the biggest impediment of project success factors is lack of respect for the time component. Once a strategic planning project is started, the planner must manage time and the client's expectation of time and resources.

## GAINING BUY-IN

Gaining buy-in is the process of raising the level of understanding to gain agreement and advocacy. The more the stakeholders advocate for the process and the subsequent plan, the more likely the plan will be successful. The easiest way to gain buy-in is first by gaining credibility, then trust and respect. If the planner can build and maintain these elements, then the stakeholders should eventually accept and hopefully advocate for the plan. It's possible to concede that some may never accept or advocate for a certain plan. For instance, if an edict comes down from leadership that all users will use Android-based tablets, then all the iPad users will probably never advocate the plan. But if they understand the reasons and economics driving the decision, they may not impede its implementation.

Buy-in is not always possible. In some projects, certain people or departments may be overtly or covertly against the project's success—especially when jobs and/or job responsibilities are at risk.

The planner would be advised not to go too far to seek buy-in from a group of naysayers. Although the more he can do to gain their trust and respect would still be worth the effort, if only to be seen as the messenger for bad news as opposed to a deliberate terminator of jobs.

When Voice over Internet Protocol (VoIP) technology was introduced, it immediately rendered the analog (and digital) phone system practically obsolete overnight. Hundreds of phone technicians in large enterprises were laid off or forced to retire as network-based telephones took their place and network engineers took over the role of voice communications.

In a VoIP cost justification project performed by their IT consulting firm for a large school district when VoIP was introduced, the resulting ROM cost model showed a $15 million cost saving over a ten-year period versus upgrading their current phones systems to a digital platform. The Telecommunications department hired their own consultant that showed the opposite impact. Thirty telecommunications jobs were on the line. The relationship between the VoIP consultant and the Telecommunications department was acrimonious at best. The board meeting to discuss this cost justification was also very exciting.

## CONSENSUS

Consensus can be gained in several ways. One way to get consensus is to say, "we can either tell them what we are planning and seek buy-in, or we can shove it down their throats, which way would you prefer?" Sometimes the latter option is actually easier.

It would not be appropriate to start a project by saying, "this is what we're going to do …" One thing that can be counted on, especially in a group of IT professionals, is that there will be dissension and objection. IT professionals like to challenge and question all things technical.

Seeking consensus is the group version of gaining buy-in. The best way to gain consensus is through education and understanding. By presenting a flow of logic beginning at a point all in the group understand to be an obvious starting point, and providing a logical flow of facts and arguments that can't be disputed, the planner can build a consensus.

The MAPIT™ planning process is that logical flow of facts. If all parties are together, and are formally presented the inputs and outputs of each phase, it will be difficult to inject objections along the way—except with technical debates. Technology debates can be heated and emotional. Whether the technology implications are truly impactful to the enterprise as a whole is not relevant. These technical debates will typically arise early in the Discovery and Needs Analysis phases, but will come to a decision point later on in the Recommendations phase where the design directions are determined and the actual Systems and Technical recommendations are defined.

### Planner Perspectives

The planner must be prepared for this debate. Whether the resolution or final decision is determined by cost, practicality, or edict, the planner must arm himself with the organization's best interest and be prepared to referee a battle among the technical staff.

At this early stage of the Needs Identification process, the planner should seek neutrality to these issues and spend time to educate himself on the technical and political debate that will likely follow.

## DISCUSSION

In any project meeting it is important to foster discussion. The planner never builds credibility or trust by shutting down dissention. It is the planner's responsibility to lead meetings to foster outcomes and objectives. Circular or off-point discussions must be directed, focused, or cut-off. Any discussion that is relevant and not openly discussed and resolved may become a festering issue that will invariably raise its ugly head at a later date, often to the detriment of the project.

For instance, think of this scenario:

> *An IT group is discussing a project to upgrade a server platform's operating system. The applications running on the server are customized for the organization. As the System Engineers discuss the upgrade process, one of the application developers says that a special API (application programing interface) will need to be upgraded first.*
>
> *If this scope change is not assimilated into the project, this issue may arise at the time of the upgrade rendering the application broken until the API is upgraded.*
>
> *The required upgrade may also affect time and cost constraints. Is it available now? What is the licensing cost?*

The planner should take note of this technical issue and keep it handy for future inclusion in the plans. He may need to return to the technical experts at a later date to obtain the specifics of the need as they apply to the Systems and Technology decisions. He must research the details of this issue and become the most informed of how this issue impacts the project plan.

## OBJECTIONS

Dealing with objections is a natural part of planning and it is the responsibility of the planner to manage and address them directly.

Objections may not always be resolved in that interaction or ever, but without addressing it and understanding it, the planner will earn an early opponent and possible saboteur.

It is important for the planner not to take sides in early discussions, but to take copious notes about the details. Oftentimes, a technical staff member may have invested significant time and resources into a project or an issue. The planner's efforts may be viewed as starting over again, diminishing the effort already taken. The astute planner will recognize this and request to leverage the work already done. The planner should take in all the data offered and decide later on relevance.

Here's a scenario:

*In a weekly status meeting of a wireless implementation project, one of the engineers objected to the type of security being implemented. The resulting discussion became an unresolved debate. The planner interjected, and said, "we'll take it under advisement."*

This objection could be handled in a couple of different ways. One way is to shut down the dispute as a nonissue. This would be a risky move for the planner unless he's armed with information justifying it or an edict stating it.

The other would be to allow the objection, take it under advisement, and allow the meeting to move toward its objective. By allowing the objection, even if it is denied in the future, the objector will have been "heard" and will be unable to say in the future that no one would listen to him.

The planner is now challenged with resolving the technical debate, either with a consensus from the engineers, or a pronouncement from leadership. He should also attempt to resolve this issue before the next status meeting. Otherwise this issue could impact resource scheduling and project initiation.

## BACKGROUND

As stated earlier, the background document is an exercise in compiling and developing copious documentation and developing a deep understanding of the client's environmental characteristics and project scope. The process of organizing, developing logical diagrams, and reviewing the written documents with the appropriate parties will require the planner to be fully immersed in the environment. It will also provide the means for the planner to engage reluctant stakeholders and gain their support and advocacy because they will be doing research into the basis of all their challenges.

Once drafted, the process of having department heads and stakeholders review the background document before moving to the Needs Analysis phase will ensure accuracy as well as advocacy.

Since the background document should be strictly fact-based, there should be no opinion or editorial. Often technical consultants forget that they may be insulting the very people reading their report. If the IT department is not using a Call Tracking software, then that is a fact; it doesn't mean the planner should state that the IT department is dysfunctional.

The Background document not only serves to lay the groundwork for the basis of the needs and project objectives, but it also serves to bring all stakeholders up to the same level of understanding of the environment relative to the project itself.

For instance, although the company president may not know the operating systems that the servers are running on, this information (if relevant to the plan) would force each stakeholder to understand the role of the operating systems, that they provide the infrastructure for the applications running on them. And that without them (and their associated costs—licenses), they may hinder or prevent the project from moving forward. When cost is involved, it is best to get these issues out in the open very early in the discovery process.

When the planner receives these types of relevant items, he must be sure to document them for all interested to see and take note. In essence, the planner becomes a sort of "tattler" on issues that may have been hidden from decision makers.

## EXISTING SYSTEMS CONFIGURATIONS

In the next section—Needs Analysis—the first of the three-layer process (Business Needs) will require a GAP analysis. The important starting point of the GAP analysis is best summed by the common computer saying, "Garbage in, garbage out." This could not be more true than in the GAP analysis. If the basic tenets, concepts, and assumptions made in the Needs Identification process are flawed, the whole plan will be flawed.

And another relentlessly true concept regarding planning is, "a butterfly flaps its wings in China and causes a hurricane in Texas." The meaning here is that even small inaccuracies or missed details in the early planning process can have catastrophic results in implementation.

For example, if during the planning of a large-scale software upgrade, the planner fails to recognize that there is an incompatibility between some of the desktop OS versions and the new software application. This could mean that when the new software is deployed, some users with older desktop OS versions may not be able to use the new application without the OS upgrade. What if half the desktops don't have enough memory for the OS upgrade? Is there time in the plan to stop while they open each desktop computer and add memory? What else may break when they start opening the desktop computers? Are the desktop computers so old that they may not turn on after the memory upgrade? Would it be more cost-effective just to get new desktops?

This detail may have evaded the planner because of lack of in-depth technical understanding, research, and also likely because of lack of testing, but if this detail is not uncovered until the actual implementation, then the delays or additional resources and budget required to save the project may be untenable.

The point of this discussion is that the deliverables from one phase of the process are the inputs for subsequent phases, and errors or omissions early in the process can handicap or kill a plan in its tracks. This is why I am constantly reinforcing the concept of "formal" processes.

Think—informal = irrelevant, formal = relevant.

## RELEVANT SYSTEMS

One of the deliverables for this process is the logical design—existing. It is incumbent of the planner to develop a logical design to best portray the relevant systems of the project to the stakeholders. This logical design consists primarily of two components but of course this will vary to the greater level as the plan complexity increases. These two primary components are the logical diagram and the design narrative.

The logical diagram is a logical (as opposed to a scaled or a physical) diagram of the relevant technology infrastructure and systems. Relevant being the key because in an accounting software upgrade, the structured cabling may likely be irrelevant to the project and out of the scope of the logical diagram. Conversely, if the new accounting software relies on wireless access as a new feature, then structured cabling and wireless networking are not only relevant but also the focus of a preliminary phase that must be completed successfully in order to perform the upgrade. Once again the planner must understand and focus the plan scope and the logical design like a laser beam.

A picture is worth a thousand words. That's why the logical diagram becomes such an important component and deliverable from the Needs Identification phase. The logical design allows all stakeholders to visualize the components and scope of the project. The focus of this diagram is to allow nontechnical types to understand the way major components fit together and depend on each other. The logical design should not be a technical diagram—it should not include information such as IP addresses or software configurations. Often the diagrams developed by System Engineers and Network Engineers include information and data that is not relevant to the stakeholders who will be viewing this logical diagram.

By including specific components and their connections and interdependencies, key concepts regarding the current topologies and system architectures can become easily understandable for nontechnical stakeholders.

For instance, in the logical diagram in figure 1.3—Logical Design 1, it is easy to visualize several things:

1. A significant amount of computing infrastructure and storage is at the District Office Data Center. If this physical location does not have secure

## Chapter One

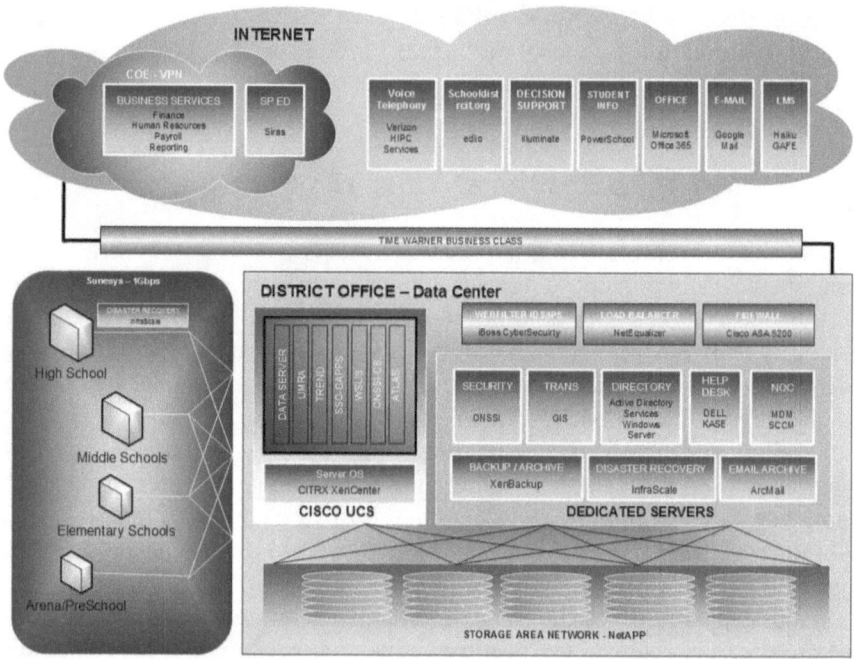

**Figure 1.3** Logical Design 1.

building envelope, security, redundant power, and air conditioning, the majority of the district's computing operation could be at risk.
2. A fairly large number of applications are in the cloud, some as paid-for services, and some through the local county office of education. This depiction shows the variety of applications the district users are accessing and likely paying for outside the district.
3. All the cloud-based applications are accessed via a single Internet connection. This architecture allows for no backup connectivity if this *one* link is compromised.
4. There may be an overlap in applications being hosted at the district and applications accessed via the cloud. Does this cause compatibility and/or training issues? What about licensing costs of duplicate applications?

By creating clear and easy to understand logical diagrams and reviewing them with stakeholders, the planner can fully understand the environment and scope, as well as allow the stakeholders to participate in the vetting and accuracy of the diagram.

Needs Identification 21

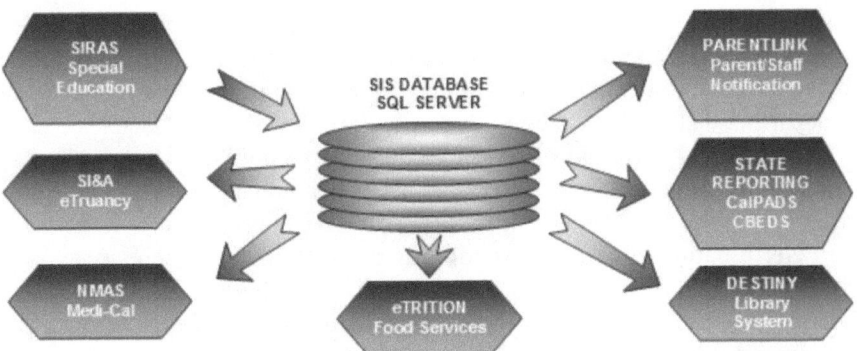

Figure 1.4 Software Logical Design.

## DESIGN NARRATIVE

Although a picture is worth a thousand words, the background document and design narrative are the thousand words. The background document deliverable from this phase must fully describe in appropriate detail the components of the systems and services in their current state, how they connect and interrelate, how they represent the "current" topology and/or architecture, and which will become the baseline for the GAP analysis in the next phase.

Once again, scope is the key. If this was a Data Center Cooling upgrade project, this logical diagram appropriately represents the criticality of the equipment and services running in the current Data Center. It is easy to understand the importance of air conditioning and backup power by seeing the services based within this critical room.

Similarly, if the scope of the project is a student information system software upgrade, none of the information of this logical diagram in figure 1.3 is relevant, and the diagram in figure 1.4 would be the correctly scoped logical diagram.

## COMPILATION

Compilation is the task of organizing all this discovery data into a concise background document that represents the collective relevant information required to support the objectives to be stated as the deliverables of the Needs Identification phase.

Compilation must focus on relevant information because often times, in the discovery process, much information is requested and often provided that becomes irrelevant under the refined scope of the project.

For instance, in the discovery for a networking equipment upgrade, a departmental leader emphasizes that the IT organization work order system is inadequate. He states that before money is spent upgrading the network, the IT department should get their customer support services in order.

As additional information is gathered and the logical design and narrative is developed, it becomes clear that this point of fact (or opinion) is irrelevant to the project. The important point is that the planner must make the determination if this information is relevant to the project plan. And even if it isn't (relevant), he has the option to include it in the discovery data to (1) assure the stakeholder that the information was acknowledged and shared and (2) that although discovered, it has no bearing on the project scope.

The planner also has the option to exclude this data at the risk of having that stakeholder criticize the project that his concerns are censored. Of course this risk is mitigated by allowing this stakeholder to review the discovery data and comment as to the relevance of the factoid. The planner could include but diminish the relevance of the comment by including it in an "interview notes" section in the Appendix.

Again it is clear that a close and constant communication between the planner and the critical stakeholders is key to continued project focus and client satisfaction—there is no such thing as overcommunication with the client. If the planner is lucky enough to have his client say, "I don't need to know the technical details," then he's done his job correctly and can now back off.

## OBJECTIVES

The final output of the Needs Identification process are the objectives. The objectives should inherently define the scope and scale of the project in general terms. I often describe the Needs Identification objectives as two or three general statements that the CEO would understand, concur with, support, and endorse.

The objectives should be developed and defined as a direct input for the high level of the next phase: Needs Analysis–Business Needs. The planner must recognize that the objectives developed at the completion of Needs Identification may need to change once getting immersed into the Needs Analysis phase. Whether a change in technical verbiage or scope and scale, the planner should be comfortable with this revision as it means that the report is becoming more focused along with the client's expectations.

These objectives must be wordsmithed to the height of efficacy. Each word should be selected to carry weight, meaning, scope, and scale. Each objective's statement should be clear, concise, and incontrovertible. Meaning, by the time the objectives have been written and approved by all the stakeholders, everyone should be in agreement to the objectives as a group and as individuals with no qualifications or exceptions.

If there are objections, allow the objectors to offer their revision, in an effort to garner their participation and endorsement. If there are qualifications or exceptions taken to the stated objectives, then it is incumbent of the planner to refine these stated objectives until all stakeholders agree and consent.

Without this buy-in process, the planner immediately exposes the plan to flaws and sabotage. By openly engaging all stakeholders, the planner eliminates the opportunities for future objections and disagreement.

There should be no more than two or three objectives—maximum. If a project requires four or more objectives, it must be rescoped or split into subprojects. For instance, if a project's objectives state the need to

- increase performance to cloud-based applications,
- address disaster recovery, and
- identify accounting software replacement,

understand that these separate projects are not directly related to each other and should be planned and managed as separate projects, in a sequence.

Although they are all components of the business, they are three objectives that address three separate needs.

## SCOPE AND SCALE

At this phase of the planning process, the planner is still looking to develop broad, all-encompassing "needs." He must resist from developing solutions or focusing on specific technologies at this early stage.

The objectives should inherently limit the scope and scale of the needs.

Let's look at some examples:

*Scenario One—Wi-Fi Implementation*

| | |
|---|---|
| Objective | Implement Mobile Computing |
| Scope | Wi-Fi implementation which may include additional switches, cabling, antennae, and control systems. |
| Scale | All school sites and district office with enough bandwidth to support every student one device (1:1). |

| Scenario Two—Student Information System (SIS) Selection | |
|---|---|
| Objectives | 1. Identify and implement new SIS system<br>2. Upgrade network and computing infrastructure to support online SIS access and mobility |
| Scope | 1. Student Information System Selection. Network Infrastructure and Wireless Saturation |
| Scale | 1. All students<br>2. All sites |

## CHAPTER ONE ESSENTIALS

1. The focus of the Needs Identification process is to discover all relevant data that exists.
2. The Needs Identification process is also the first opportunity to introduce participants and stakeholders to the logic of the process, to build credibility in the methodology, and trust in the planner.
3. The core inputs should include the school's approved and accepted educational and strategic goals as they may call for the need of systems and technology.
4. The outputs of the Needs Identification process are the background document and the objectives.
5. There should be no more than two to three objectives.
6. The objectives should be generalized, all-encompassing, and incontrovertible.

*Chapter Two*

# Needs Analysis

The second phase of the MAPIT™ Planning methodology is Needs Analysis (figure 2.1). In this phase, a three-layered, top-down, granular approach is used to detail and understand the component "needs" of the scope and objectives delivered in the Needs Identification phase.

It should be noted that while a significant part of the first phase is interaction with the client, stakeholders, department heads, and staff, the Needs Analysis phase is the part where the consultants "go away for a while" to come up with things and then come back and review each of these three levels of needs. The things they come up with will then be used to form the basis of the recommendations in the next phase.

The three-layered model for Needs Analysis are: Business Needs, Systems Needs, and Technical Needs. As applied to education, the Business Needs might be renamed as Educational Needs (schools are in the business of education).

A simple way of looking at this is:

1. Educational Needs are what the superintendent thinks he needs,
2. Systems Needs are what the assistant superintendent of business thinks the superintendent needs, and
3. Technical Needs are what the director of IT thinks they need.

This analysis must occur from the top down. Why? Because all plans, tasks, and efforts must be developed in support of the Educational Needs. Remember, the Educational Needs are a restatement of the objectives defined in the Needs Identification phase.

The Systems Needs and Technical Needs only exist to support the Educational Needs. Once again, the planner must keep his analytical mind

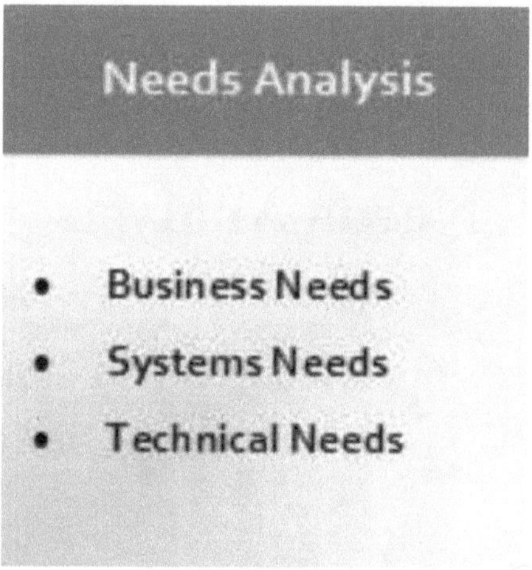

**Needs Analysis**

- Business Needs
- Systems Needs
- Technical Needs

**Figure 2.1  Needs Analysis Process**

focused on needs and not solutions throughout this process. And once again, this does not mean that the planner couldn't likely make an educated guess or prediction, it just warrants the full depth of analysis before taking those next steps. If all the steps are followed correctly and passed before the review committee at every milestone, it will be very difficult to raise objections later in the process.

In other words, naming and identifying Educational Needs is a way of "wrapping yourself with the flag." Acknowledging that the needs of the school board and the superintendent drive all the subsequent planning is both a nod to leadership and a badge of credibility (figure 2.2).

## EDUCATIONAL (BUSINESS) NEEDS

Once again, it's easy to think of Educational needs as what the superintendent thinks he needs. The superintendent doesn't think to himself, "we need VMware," which would be a technical need. In fact, it can be seen that the superintendent is at least two tiers removed from such a thought. Superintendents of schools tend to think of student performance, equity, school operations, safety, and so on. All these can be stated as Educational Needs. It is then the job of the planner to apply the Educational Needs to the scope and scale of the objectives.

Returning to our two scenarios (see tables 2.1 and 2.2).

From Scenario Two, it can be seen that each objective breeds its own set of needs. In this case, a new Student Information System (SIS) that includes

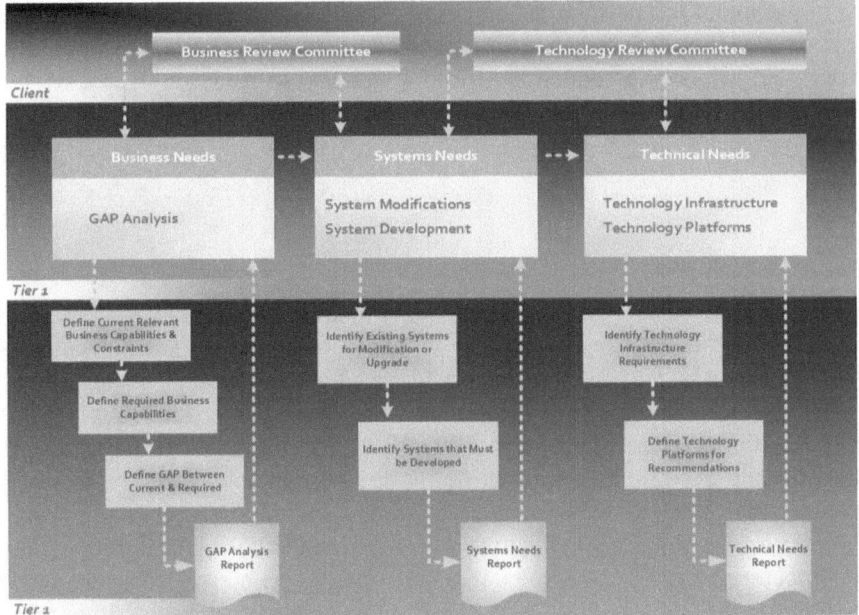

**Figure 2.2** Needs Analysis Breakout.

**Table 2.1 Scenario One—Wi-Fi Implementation: Educational Needs**

| | |
|---|---|
| Objective | Implement Wi-Fi throughout all sites to support 1:1 computing. |
| Scope | Wi-Fi which may include additional switches, cabling, antennae, and control systems. |
| Scale | All sites, with enough bandwidth to support every student one device (1:1). |
| Educational Need | All curriculum must be accessible to each student online. |

**Table 2.2 Scenario Two—Student Information System (SIS) Selection: Educational Needs**

| | |
|---|---|
| Objectives | 1. Identify and implement new SIS system<br>2. Upgrade network and computing infrastructure to support online SIS access and mobility. |
| Scope | 1. SIS Selection<br>2. Network Infrastructure and Wireless Saturation |
| Scale | 1. All students<br>2. All sites |
| Educational Needs | 1. The staff must have access to all student information to comply with federal and state reporting, testing as well as all relevant personal and academic data.<br>2. The district network must support robust wired and wireless computing in order to access the SIS. |

mobility apps for smartphones and tablets will trigger a network upgrade to support mobility. In a large enterprise, this project would have to be split into individual projects in sequence. But in a smaller- to medium-sized environment, these two interrelated projects could be planned and managed as a single initiative.

## GAP ANALYSIS

The GAP analysis is exactly what its name means. I guess it really shouldn't be capitalized but it seems to be the common designation. The GAP analysis is defined as the area between a given current state and some defined future state. For MAPIT™ Planning, the current state is defined in the Needs Identification process. The deliverables from the phase include the logical diagram and design narrative that define the current state of relevant architectures and systems—designated "Current Technology Architecture" and the proposed future state of technology—designated "Proposed Technology Architecture." Once again, relevance becomes a subjective judgment made by the planner, but scope and scale definitions of the project will aid in these judgments.

So, how to define this "future" state? Keep in mind that the planner is still on the "needs" side of the planning process. So, that means that this future state must also be defined in the form of needs.

The best way to initiate this part of the Needs Analysis is to start with the "Current Technology Architecture" logical diagram. The logical diagram developed in the Needs Identification process should provide a basis for the future state or "Proposed Technology Architecture." For instance, in the Wi-Fi Implementation scenario, a correctly depicted logical diagram might reflect none or minimal wireless infrastructure.

For the future or "Proposed" network, new equipment in the form of a wireless controller, additional power-over Ethernet switches, and wireless antennae would be depicted. Go ahead and utilize this proposed logical diagram as a basis for discussion and acceptance because it will become a key deliverable in the form of Systems Design that will be developed in the next phase, Recommendations.

As the planner moves from the Needs Analysis phase to Recommendations, then to feasibility, the final Systems Design will be borne of this Proposed Technology Architecture and will continue to evolve with each new identified technology, system, and product.

One can see that as the planner moves along in the process, he will likely have to go back and make revisions. For instance, there might be a need to add the old equipment to the existing systems drawing in order to depict the new equipment in the proposed systems drawing. For this reason, all the documents and deliverables published and distributed for review should be marked as DRAFT—DO NOT DISTRIBUTE in the header or footer of EVERY page in order to keep open the opportunity to revise without amending to FINAL documents. Secondly, the date should also be embedded to provide a version control for these DRAFT documents.

Once the Proposed Technology Architecture logical diagram is developed, the associated proposed design narrative can detail the elements of the proposed configuration and finally the GAP analysis report.

Once again, the planner is reminded that the gap is defined as Educational Needs that will then become the inputs to the next layer of Needs Analysis—Systems Needs. The outputs of this subprocess are the Current Technology Architecture, the Proposed Technology Architecture, and the GAP analysis report. Also note that the Proposed Technology Architecture diagram must be revised because it will eventually become the graphic depiction for the Strategic Technology Plan proposed Systems Design and Tactical Implementation Plan(s).

## Planner Perspectives

It is common practice to utilize only hard-copy printouts for these frequent interactions with the clients. Distributing electronic copies of draft reports risks sharing and publication of documents that have not been finalized. In addition to clearly marking all pages with DRAFT—DO NOT DISTRIBUTE, and the date, controlling the sharing of hard-copy documents is much easier and less obtrusive to all parties—albeit a waste of paper. It is also a wise practice to provide all the printed documents to the meeting participants and to collect them at the end. If someone has marked up the copy with notes or wants to keep it, the DRAFT designation and date will reinforce that the documents are not be shared and are not final.

## SYSTEMS NEEDS

*System* may be one of the most innocuous words used by everyone every day. But for our purposes, systems are a combination of technology hardware, software, infrastructure, and processes that provide a business service to an organization.

Systems Needs fall into two categories: modifications and development. The planner, from his intimate understanding of the technical environment developed through the Needs Identification phase, must make determinations if current systems will be modified or upgraded, or will an entirely new system be planned and implemented. This question and determination should be vetted by all interested parties, it is not a decision the planner should make on his own without guidance unless he himself is the significant technical expert.

For instance, in line with our scenarios, the Wi-Fi upgrade is an upgrade of the wireless network infrastructure, equipment, and control software that become the wireless infrastructure for the mobile devices (table 2.3). Stated as a System Need, the organization needs a wireless network that provides mobility and access for the student devices.

As the planner seeks to finalize the Systems Needs and develop and review options for technologies and Technical Needs, he will begin to identify if the current systems will be upgraded or whether new systems will be developed (table 2.4).

Table 2.3   Scenario One—Wi-Fi Implementation: System Needs

| | |
|---|---|
| Objective | Implement Wi-Fi throughout all sites to support 1:1 computing. |
| Scope | Wi-Fi which may include additional switches, cabling, antennae, and control systems. |
| Scale | All sites, with enough bandwidth to support every student one device (1:1). |
| Business Need | All online curriculum must be accessible to each student using a mobile device. |
| System Need | All sites require wireless network infrastructure, equipment, and control software to support student device mobility. |

Table 2.4   Scenario Two—Student Information System (SIS) Selection: System Needs

| | |
|---|---|
| Objectives | 1. Identify and implement new SIS system<br>2. Upgrade network and computing infrastructure to support online SIS access and mobility. |
| Scope | 1. SIS Selection<br>2. Network Infrastructure and Wireless Saturation |
| Scale | 1. All students<br>2. All sites |
| Business Needs | 1. The district must have access to all student information to comply with federal and state reporting, testing as well as all relevant personal and academic data.<br>2. The district network must support robust wired and wireless computing in order to access the SIS. |
| Systems Needs | 1. The district requires a SIS that addresses all the Business Needs.<br>2. The district network system requires additional infrastructure, equipment, and software to support SIS application performance and mobility. |

At this point the planner must begin to make assumptions, deductions, and decisions based on his clear understanding of the GAP analysis. Each of these assumption, deductions, and decisions should be made with key stakeholders' understanding and endorsement. For instance, the Wi-Fi engineer should endorse the decision made on wireless security, while the facilities manager would endorse the data center fire suppression system.

Based on the current systems architecture and the GAP requirements, the planner must begin to understand if the current systems require modifications or upgrades, or will entirely new systems be required.

It is quite possible that this determination can't be made at this point. For instance, in Scenario One—Wi-Fi Implementation, the planner might need to determine if the current network will need upgrades or modifications, versus installing all new cabling and equipment.

The MAPIT™ methodology guides the planner to base all assumptions, deductions, and decisions to be made in pursuit of the best-case scenario—as if money were no object. This process is called "Blue Sky" planning. Blue Sky, because it is an effort to root the planning in the best practices, the industry standard, the ideal solution.

Here is one test: if the Blue Sky plan does not accomplish all the project objectives identified in the Needs Identification process, then the project must be rescoped with new objectives. If the Blue Sky plan doesn't fulfill all the requirements of all the stakeholders, the project is doomed to fail—if not in the eyes of all, surely in the eyes of some.

At this early stage of the project planning process, any assumptions, deductions, or decisions that aren't in pursuit of the best-case scenario are prematurely constrained. Meaning that any decision to limit the capacity or diminish the scope of the project is based on no specific limiting factor—just the planner's instinct, or the client's bias.

Unless this determination of modification versus development is clearly understood by all parties and stakeholders at the review stage, then it is contingent upon the planner to carry the planning process through recommendations and allow the feasibility study to provide the constraints of scope, time, and cost. What does this complex sentence mean? It means stick with the Blue Sky solution all the way through to the feasibility study.

For instance, once again in Scenario One—Wi-Fi Implementation, it might be discovered in the GAP analysis that the current structured cabling could support bandwidth up to 1 Gbps but not 10 Gbps and that the equipment would support an upgrade to 10 Gbps. That would mean the plan could pursue a design objective to upgrade to 1 Gbps for $100,000 and that a new installation of cabling to support a 10 Gbps upgrade would cost $500,000 (500 percent more!). It would be presumptive of the planner not to pursue the

10 Gpbs upgrade unless he knew in advance that only $100,000 of funding is available, which again, may be premature, subject to a full feasibility study.

The point being, this early determination between modification and development will be reviewed with the client committee for validation. The planner does not and should not stick his neck out on an early determination. If anything, the planner should be advocating for the Blue Sky solution until he's absolutely forced to compromise or limit the scope, scale, or technology.

There are, however, some instances where the determination is obvious or predirected. For instance, if there is no existing structured cabling infrastructure and new construction is being funded, then obviously, the planning is for new development. Similarly, if in Scenario One they were only looking to go to 1 Gbps for the near term, then the client stakeholder may predetermine that this element is restricted to the short-term objective.

## SYSTEMS MODIFICATION

Systems Modification refers to the modification or upgrade to current or existing systems. These modifications or upgrades may be hardware, software (licenses), practices, services (cloud-based), or any combination of these.

In this section of the Needs Analysis phase, the planner will utilize his intimate understanding of the current technologies and architectures to deduce and determine if the Blue Sky solution set would call for a modification to the current system or a completely new system. This will also have a significant impact to the third granular level of the Needs Analysis—Technical Needs.

Once a preliminary determination has been made (preliminarily subject to feasibility), then the planner can begin to develop the Technical Needs.

## SYSTEMS DEVELOPMENT

Systems Development refers to new systems implementation. Oftentimes, new systems are easiest to design and implement but more costly than upgrades. New systems may be defined when the Business Needs call for a type of system capability that doesn't already exist within the organization, or when existing systems cannot facilitate an upgrade that supports the business requirements. New systems can be hardware, software (licenses), processes, procedures as well as cloud-based and/or hosted services, or any combination of these.

Once these determinations are made, then the planner will utilize the Systems Needs information to begin defining Technical Needs.

## TECHNICAL NEEDS

Once the planner has reached this point in the Needs Analysis, he is well on the way to develop a preliminary solution set based on the Blue Sky solution or some kind of prequalified solution. The process of identifying and defining Technical Needs may become very daunting as a single Systems Need may trigger a complex string of Technical Needs. This is the main reason it was stated in the Needs Identification phase that the objectives should not exceed three. One or two is preferred. And here's why, once the planner gets to the technical details, each objective will become one or more Educational Needs.

Each Educational Need may become one or more Systems Needs. And each Systems Need will dictate a string of Technical Needs.

For instance, the Mobility Educational Need described in Scenario One—Wi-Fi Implementation will trigger a Wireless Network Systems Need, which would entail Technical Needs including construction, power upgrades, and cabling installation in addition to the new equipment specific for the wireless network.

So what started as a simple generalized, all-encompassing stated goal, gives rise to a long list of tasks and activities to build and deliver infrastructure and the proposed solution set. And the planner must keep documenting each phase as he goes along, both to record the history of the decision-making process and the evolution of the solution set. All this documentation will preserve the what and why's of the final proposed solution architecture.

The new software need discussed in Scenario Two—SIS Selection will not only require the software and associated hardware platform(s) which may also include computing and storage hardware, but will also encompass all the Systems Needs in Scenario One because it also requires Mobility just as in Scenario One—Wi-Fi Implementation.

## TECHNOLOGY INFRASTRUCTURE

Technical Needs will likely be divided into two sections: infrastructure and platforms.

Technology infrastructure refers to the lower levels of the OSI model: Physical, Data Link, Network, Transport, and Session. These layers address technology systems that are required for basic networking and computing such as cabling, network equipment (switches, routers), wireless control, network (domain) and computing management systems, and connectivity to the Internet.

Network and computing services may also fall into the infrastructure section if they are assumed or required in support of a higher-level application. For instance, if a new electronic mail service is the business need, then the Internet connectivity, local-area network, and supporting technologies are the infrastructure, while the new servers, operating system, and e-mail application constitute the platform. Alternately, if a new SIS system must synchronize with a directory service, then that directory service is actually infrastructure required to support the new SIS system.

This should not be a labored decision; some projects may not have infrastructure separate from a platform. Or, the platform may require an infrastructure that is 100 percent in place, so the infrastructure component is not part of the planning process.

## TECHNOLOGY PLATFORMS

Thus, the Technology Infrastructure and Platforms address the Technical Needs for the objective. The needs that directly address the Systems Needs. Technical Needs, or technologies, that support a "system" may be generalized and defined with industry standards, such as 802.11ac or ODBC compliant. Or they may be manufacturer-specific, and likely proprietary, such as AppleTV or Cisco Call Manager.

For instance, if the technical need is wireless network equipment based on 802.11ac, there are several manufacturers competing in this space; however, if the organization is standardized on a proprietary platform, then the technology need may also be manufacturer-specific.

Imagine the Wi-Fi Implementation Blue Sky recommendation is determined to move to the 10 Gbps upgrade triggering the Technical Needs given in table 2.5.

One can see by the sheer number of subordinate Technical Needs that the number can grow exponentially. For instance, in a multischool or multibuilding campus, such as a large high school or hospital, each facility may require a separate project plan for the facilities upgrade over time. Of course, the priority and phasing of the projects and subprojects have not even been considered at this point in the planning.

Once again, the planner is reminded that he is still on the needs side of the solution set. As he considers the Technical Needs above, he can see that some needs require specific technologies. For instance, the Systems need to support mobility for a large-scale population of students warrants the assumed Blue Sky requirement to upgrade core networking performance to the current state-of-the-art technology—10 Gbps. This bandwidth can only be supported by OM4-rated fiber-optic backbone cabling. How is this determined? The

**Table 2.5  Scenario One—Wi-Fi Implementation: Technical Needs**

| | |
|---|---|
| Objective | Implement Wi-Fi throughout all sites to support 1:1 computing. |
| Scope | Wi-Fi which may include additional switches, cabling, antennae, and control systems. |
| Scale | All sites, with enough bandwidth to support every student one device (1:1). |
| Business Need | All online curriculum must be accessible to each student using a mobile device. |
| System Need | All sites require wireless network infrastructure, equipment, and control software to support student device mobility. |
| Technical Needs | 1. Structured Cabling<br>   a. New main distribution frame (MDF) and intermediate distribution frame (IDF) facilities upgrades capable of supporting new structured cabling and associated power, racks, and enclosures.<br>   b. New MDF and IDF power upgrades<br>      i. May require new survey, transformers, and ducting<br>   c. New pathways, trenching, and conduit installation between MDF and IDF closets.<br>   d. New fiber-optic backbone cabling (OM4)<br>   e. New copper-horizontal cabling (Cat6)<br>2. Network Equipment (10 Gbps)<br>   a. Core switches<br>   b. Edge switches<br>   c. VoIP phones<br>3. Wi-Fi Equipment<br>   a. Wireless Controllers<br>   b. Wireless Control Systems (Servers and Management suite)<br>   c. Wireless Access Points (WAPs). |

planner once again uses the OSI model to determine the needs. Starting at the top down, the planner will see the need for wireless management at the application layer, but will then skip several layers down to the Network layer where the 10 Gpbs specification is encountered.

Once the component Technical Needs are determined at this layer, then the planner can move down to the Data Link and the Physical layer where 90 percent of the planning and implementation will occur for this project. It's the installation of this new cabling between buildings that will trigger the requirements for new pathways and facilities to accommodate the new cabling.

As another important consideration, the planner can't assume that the legacy infrastructure can be demolished or removed from production before any upgrades are initiated, what would be called a *hard cutover*. A hard cutover would mean that the network and systems would be out of operation during the demolition and deployment of the new systems. Typically this cannot be accommodated without a hard downtime window, like several days out of production.

So, since a hard cutover and the associated downtime are not possible, that means that a *migration* will be the cutover method—which means that the two systems will run parallel for a while.

What are the implications of running the two systems parallel? Don't toy with this issue. Running parallel systems can disrupt the integrity of existing processes, procedures, and people dependent on these systems. What if the new system comes online while the legacy system has not been taken out of production? What if some users use the old system while others use the new systems? It becomes clear to the planner that communication and training will be the key to his program's success. Something to be managed closely by the project manager when these projects start to go into the implementation mode.

In fact, it is more realistic to assume that the legacy systems will never be removed, which will trigger the need for additional new facilities to accommodate all new cabling, both fiber-optic backbone and copper horizontal. Unless the budget is also big enough to include demolition and removal (labor) of legacy infrastructure, it probably will never happen.

In a large defense contractor in the 1990s, whenever new cabling was installed under the data center raised floor, it was too risky to attempt to remove the old cabling. So the cable heads were simply cut off and the old cabling was left under the floor. Imagine what it's like under that floor today.

The planner must be very careful to engage with Subject Matter Experts (SMEs) during the definition of each Technical Need. In practice, the best SMEs are the actual trade people and estimators. The planner shouldn't assume that he can use the same estimating technique as his contractors. Especially when facilities such as main distribution frame (MDF) and intermediate distribution frame (IDF) rooms and cabling pathways and conduits are concerned. The planner should not make these deductions and assumptions unless he is actually the one in charge of the construction and hiring the labor for pulling the cable.

Even the assumption that pathways are in place is ill conceived. This fact cannot be established without a survey performed by a qualified cabling installation contractor, preferably the one doing the actual installation. Unless there is pull string in place in an open conduit, the planner better assume that trenching and new conduits between buildings will be required.

Considering the Technical Needs of Scenario Two—SIS Selection (table 2.6), the planner will quickly see that if the network and wireless infrastructure is not in place to support student and teacher mobility, then the network infrastructure component of this scenario is exactly the same as Scenario One—Wi-Fi Implementation because a full Wi-Fi network is required to support the SIS system's mobility features.

**Table 2.6  Scenario Two—Student Information System (SIS) Selection: Technical Needs**

| | |
|---|---|
| Objectives | 1. Identify and implement new SIS system<br>2. Upgrade network and computing infrastructure to support online SIS access and mobility. |
| Scope | 1. SIS Selection<br>2. Network Infrastructure and Wireless Saturation |
| Scale | 1. All students<br>2. All sites |
| Business Needs | 1. The district must have access to all student information to comply with federal and state reporting, testing as well as all relevant personal and academic data.<br>2. The district network must support robust wired and wireless computing in order to access the SIS. |
| Systems Needs | 1. The district requires a SIS that addresses all the Business Needs.<br>2. The district network system requires additional infrastructure, equipment and software to support SIS application performance and mobility. |
| Technical Needs | 1. New SIS System—System Selection Process<br>  a. Required Feature Set<br>2. Structured Cabling<br>  a. New main distribution frame (MDF) and intermediate distribution frame (IDF) facilities upgrades capable of supporting new structured cabling and associated power, racks and enclosures.<br>  b. New MDF and IDF power upgrades<br>    i. May require new survey, transformers, ducting<br>  c. New pathways, trenching and conduit installation between MDF and IDF closets.<br>  d. New fiber-optic backbone cabling (OM4)<br>  e. New copper-horizontal cabling (Cat6)<br>3. Network Equipment (10 Gbps)<br>  a. Core switches<br>  b. Edge switches<br>  c. VoIP phones<br>4. Wi-Fi Equipment<br>  a. Wireless Controllers<br>  b. Wireless Control Systems (Servers and Management suite)<br>  c. Wireless Access Points (WAPs). |

## CHAPTER TWO ESSENTIALS

1. The primary inputs are the Needs Identification outputs: Background Document and the Objectives.
2. The process of performing interviews, research, and compilation of the discovery data creates the planner's basis for developing an intimate

understanding of the client's environment enough to carry the planning process forward.
3. The planner should never give the impression that he knows more than the client about his own environment.
4. The GAP analysis will be based on the current technology logical diagram developed in the Needs Identification process.
5. The outputs are Systems Needs, Technical Needs, and the Gap analysis report.

*Chapter Three*

# Recommendations

The real, or original, name of this phase was Preliminary Recommendations. Why preliminary? Because these recommendations are based on the Blue Sky planning approach. The approach to pursue the industry-standard, best practice solution set that has not yet been studied for feasibility, is sometimes misunderstood by the client. He might ask the planner, "Why would we use that technology when we know we can't afford it?" To which the planner will respond, "How do you know you can't afford it? Shouldn't we make sure we can't afford the best solution before compromising it? Shouldn't we make our best effort to convince leadership to invest in the best solution?"

There is nothing worse than moving toward a compromised solution and have a top decision-maker say, "Why aren't we doing it the same way GM would do it?" In which case the planner would give the lame answer, "well I didn't think it you'd go for it." Or worse yet—and the planner should never say this, "that's what your guy told me."

Some planners may feel uncomfortable creating designs, and developing budgets for systems and technologies that the organization may not be able to afford, but not doing so would set limitations and constraints into place that may not be recognized until a much later date. For instance, the engineer may decide to install Category 5e cable instead of installing the latest Category 6 cable to save approximately 20 percent on the cable. What this decision doesn't take into account is that the materials and labor to install the higher-grade cable are pretty much the same, and these may total more than half of the installation. Meaning that even though the cabling costs 20 percent more, it might only impact the total project cost by 5 percent, yet the long-range impact would be to limit the bandwidth potential by ten times. Meaning instead of being able to run 10 Gbps to each wireless antennae, the cable would be limited to 1 Gbps.

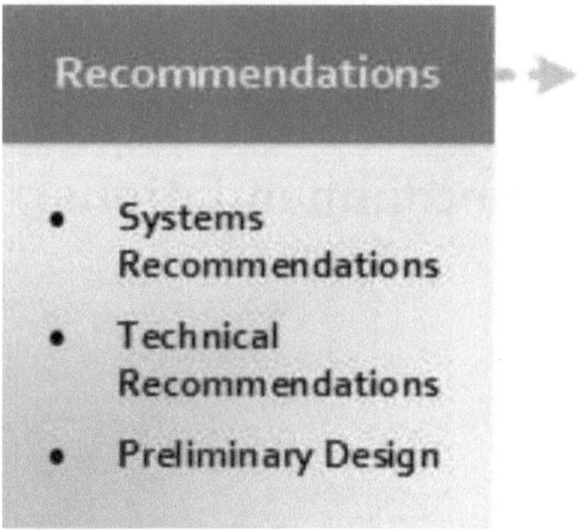

**Figure 3.1** Recommendations.

Recommendations
- Systems Recommendations
- Technical Recommendations
- Preliminary Design

It becomes more clear that this phase and effort to design the Blue Sky solution is not ill conceived. In fact, it's an absolute necessity. How will the organization ever know if it cannot afford something if the real cost is never developed and studied for feasibility? Oftentimes during the discovery and analysis phases, the planner will be having a discussion with the IT guy or a department head about possible strategies and solutions, and the client will remark, "Oh, that will never happen." Or, "they'll never go for that," or "that would cost way too much." The planner should always respond with, "How do you know?"

Well, the reality is, unless someone has done the exhaustive study, developed the strategy (with their advocacy along the way), and presented a complete report and cost model, they might be willing to spend a lot more than what they might commit to in an annual budget meeting or quarterly update.

Once the Blue Sky solution is developed, it must be reviewed and confirmed that it would truly achieve the objectives stated in the Needs Identification phase. If not, what does it mean? *It means that the most optimistic, best practice Blue Sky solution still wouldn't achieve the objectives and that this project plan will likely be doomed to failure.* At least in the eyes of some.

If this happens, the planner must acknowledge this inability to achieve the objectives and restate or revise the objectives to be achievable. Full stop—return to phase 1 and do it right this time! This might mean to get the right people on-board earlier in the process. Sorry, the planner will need to tell the client that he has to back up, without charging them for those hours.

Imagine a builder constructing a house but trying to save on cost, so the decision is made to use lower-grade materials because it will be cheaper.

Then the house falls down because of the compromise in materials, but the builder never really knew the true cost of using the right materials. He just assumed it would be cheaper and didn't pursue it further. If he did analyze the cost of doing it right, how much would it affect the overall project cost? Five percent, ten percent? And if he did do the cost analysis, would he have made the additional effort to obtain the right materials?

Just as the Needs Analysis has a layered approach of Business (Educational) Needs, Systems Needs, and Technical Needs, the Recommendations phase includes, Systems Requirements and Technical Requirements that will drive the planner toward a Preliminary Design. Once again, the design is Preliminary because it has not been studied for feasibility yet. This preliminary design becomes the primary input for the feasibility study in the next step. The deliverables are the Proposed Logical Design (which resulted from the GAP analysis) and the Preliminary Recommendations.

The Recommendations phase is the first phase where the planner makes the move from *needs* to *solutions*. This transition of thought context is very important. It is common for the planner, in the early stages, to jump to solutions and take steps toward design. But, by keeping the focus on needs, it allows the planner to perform an exhaustive study to identify and analyze these needs, and at least three opportunities to review, revise, and validate these needs with the stakeholders.

## PLANNER PERSPECTIVES

Oftentimes during these reviews, the planner may find that he actually knows more about the client's environment (in some aspects) than many of the stakeholders. The planner is warned to be very careful with this knowledge. One—he doesn't know everything. Two—he is an outsider.

He cannot intimate to the stakeholders that he is more informed than they. He can appear that he has done an extensive research, so that he has an intimate knowledge, but this is one area where clients and stakeholders may feel threatened by an outsider with more information than they have. The planner must always appear to empower his clients and stakeholders with the benefit of his research, and never appear to protect or shield them from his discovery and data.

The more the stakeholders identified during the early stages, the more important it is for the planner to seek agreement and validation. Any stakeholder left out of these review milestones before moving to solution development may become a project plan liability. Any decisions or assumptions made without validation could cause a key stakeholder to revoke his support.

Nothing is worse than reporting in a status meeting that a decision was made, and one of the key participants says, "Wait a minute, when did you make that decision?" Or worse yet, "Who made that decision?" The planner will hope one of the other stakeholders will pipe in and claim responsibility, otherwise he will be the one explaining and hopefully the one not pointing a finger at someone else!

## SYSTEM RECOMMENDATIONS

Once again, the process is a granular, top-down approach to begin to make design recommendations. And although the planner has now passed to the *solutions* phase, he must still be methodical and take each step in sequence, separately.

At the *Systems Recommendations* level, the planner has now crossed the bridge from defining needs to recommending solutions. At this level, the solutions are SYSTEMS—a combination of hardware, software (licenses), processes, and resources—that address the Systems Needs defined in the previous Needs Analysis phase.

Although the Needs Analysis phase delivers at the highest level Business Needs, the highest level of the recommendations will directly address the Systems Needs, one level down. The Business Needs are basically a restatement of the objectives in a format that allows systems to be defined to address them.

The Systems Recommendations will be developed from the following inputs:

1. Systems Needs
2. Current and relevant technology standards
3. Industry standards and best practices
4. Existing infrastructure and equipment.

All of these inputs should have been gathered and documented in the Needs Identification phase and should already be semiorganized and documented. If they aren't, the planner skipped something in the Needs Identification phase called Compilation.

### Planner Perspectives

Break—I hope you didn't think to yourself, that's just a bunch of busywork, it's a waste of time. It isn't necessary. You couldn't be more wrong. The process of creating logical designs, writing the narratives, and organizing the materials into a cohesive study is a process that endows the planner with the depth of understanding of the environment in order to make recommendations.

The process of developing a report, stating facts, and developing charts forces the creator to do extensive research, check validity and compatibility, refer to experts and manufacturers, and then review this material iteratively with the client and technical staff.

The only reason the planner has the capacity and knowledge to lead the Recommendations phase, is directly because of his intimate understanding of the environment, organizational culture, stated goals, and defined objectives. In essence, the planner becomes the Subject Matter Expert (SME) through the Needs Identification and Needs Analysis phases and must leverage this knowledge and credibility in order to present recommendations and plans.

Re-stated, the planner will not be recognized as the expert and have credibility proposing solutions, unless he has done the in-depth research and study to have the client recognize him as an expert.

## DESIGN DIRECTION

These four inputs will provide the design direction for this section of Recommendations. Using the Systems Needs defined in the Needs Analysis phase, the second and third inputs are referenced to define the general direction of the system architecture based on the fourth input.

For example, if the current organization is standardized on Cisco networking equipment, and this equipment has served well, and continues to be an industry standard, then it would be common practice to begin developing systems recommendations based on this standard.

However, if "cost effective" is mentioned anywhere in the first two phases of this planning process, it might be appropriate to ask the question at this stage:

"Should we be looking for a more cost-effective manufacturer for this system?" Or played out another way, the superintendent of a school district might say, "I heard Cisco is overpriced, why do we use it?" To which someone better be ready to offer one of these two responses:

1. It's a board approved district standard. Should we be looking at other platforms instead?

   OR

2. For this planning process, we'll be looking at how much more it costs so we can make an informed decision.

*Nonproprietary* can also be a factor in design direction. If, for some reason, an influential stakeholder or board member is told that Apple or Cisco are proprietary platforms and should be avoided, then a full review may be warranted.

Many other internal or external factors may drive a design direction during this solution development process. It will be the responsibility of the planner to vet all logical alternatives before moving down a specific pathway or solution set. And the planner's best method of mitigating design-direction mistakes is to stay in constant communication with many stakeholders.

Many being a keyword. Oftentimes, a consultant or planner engages closest with his key contact and becomes biased to the opinions of this stakeholder. However, this key contact may not be a key decision-maker or key stakeholder, so the planner must share his progress and design directions with as many stakeholders as possible through this process, gathering an audience of supporters as he goes about asking for valuable input.

It would be a fatal flaw for the planner to go away, then return with a completed plan that hadn't been vetted or approved by any stakeholders. This would simply be the path to plan limbo. The place, plans that aren't based in reality go, so people can forget about them: usually in a file cabinet of the poor soul that paid the bill.

In a more complex project where manufacturer or industry standards aren't driving a design, then a separate subproject comparing alternative technology approaches and designs may be warranted. This might be referred to as a "Comparative Technologies Study" and it is warranted whenever there are distinct alternatives with no clear technical or political factors biasing the design. This study would require preliminary designs for each alternative and a ROM cost model.

Hopefully, the planner anticipated this possible additional consulting work when proposing this planning engagement. It wouldn't be wise to go back to the client and ask for more money because the planner didn't expect to have to do this study.

For instance, in the early days of wide-area networking (WAN), circa 1990s, there were a variety of telecommunications services and architectures that could provide long-distance telecommunications, none nearly at the bandwidth available today. So companies looking at making this expenditure had to do a lot of research and comparison of technologies and associated costs. In fact, the cost models were very complex because many of the telecom services at the time (as today) required both installation and monthly service charges, which were charged and discounted very differently. Then depending on the technology, the owner would be responsible for having the appropriate facilities and equipment to connect to that technology interface.

Analog, T-1, Broadband, Microwave, Frame Relay, Fiber Distributed Data Interface (FDDI), and Multiprotocol Label Switching (MPLS) were available, all providing options for building a WAN to connect remote sites using different architectures. This would be a perfect example where comparative technologies and ROM cost model report would be in order.

Today, this example still applies except the bandwidths are 1,000 to 10,000 times greater and the technologies are "mostly" standardized on "Ethernet" protocols.

For a recent school district, planners did a comparison of technologies between Dark Fiber, Leased Fiber, and Provider Services at 10 Gbps and up to 100 Gbps. Each option required a complete logical design (overlaid on a scaled map) and a description of technology growth and expansion, both in performance as well as geographical. This study was done independently of a separate planning process. However, the resulting ROM cost models were then used as direct inputs for design direction in a later plan recommendations.

Of the four inputs numbers two and three are not absolute. Meaning that existing standards may be outdated and industry-best practices may not be applicable. For example, school boards don't often act to accept manufacturer's platforms as policy or standards. But this must be done in instances where a specific, even proprietary, technology is implemented, such as Apple computers or Novell networking systems from past. Then, as time and technology moves on, if these standards are not updated and addressed, they could become a significant obstacle to be addressed by a project manager.

## Planner Perspectives

Ultimately, the design direction must be a consensus of the most important stakeholders, not driven by biases of the planner himself. In fact, the planner should never been seen as injecting technology or manufacturer biases into the client's planning process. Expertise is one thing, bias is another.

This is where the planner may find himself in the middle of technical and political battles. It is best for the planner to seek the most likely successful pathway as he engages with as many important stakeholders and begins to lay the groundwork for the design direction. He cannot be seen to be invested in any particular solution—although he may be.

The planner is best advised not to take sides during these technical or political battles. Provide the decision-makers, technical staff, and objectors as much technical and cost information as possible and stand on the sidelines as they fight their battles.

Allegiance to manufacturers or vendors cannot play into these planning sessions for the planner to stay completely objective. This doesn't mean that the planner must absolve himself of expertise and opinion, only that he should move deliberately and carefully. Sometimes doing the right thing can still get a person fired, especially a consultant! There are instances where the planner's expertise and experience may force him to take a position on a system or technology.

For example, if the planner has had a previous wireless security method hacked, he may strongly recommend on design-direction based on this experience. He must also understand that he does so at the peril of his engagement.

## ROUGH ORDER MAGNITUDE COST MODELING

Unfortunately, it is out of the scope of this technology planning book to include a full detailed discussion about Rough Order Magnitude (ROM) cost modeling, but this book can certainly lay the groundwork. Cost modeling and budget development can be of the most complex yet important "guesses" a strategic planner may ever make—and forgive the use of the word "guesses." The process of developing ROM cost models is once again, iterative.

For MAPIT™, two to three budget estimates will likely be created through the duration of the planning (ROM1, ROM2, and ROM3). Each ROM estimate will become more accurate and more encompassing. As stakeholders participate in the iterative review process, the cost model will likely bounce up and down. The planner must keep in mind that various stakeholders and contacts will have differing perspectives of budget. Departmental staff know about their departmental budgets but rarely have insight into the actual organizational budgets.

Within the IT realm, most IT departments feel overworked and under resourced. There are only a few examples of organizations where IT budgets are not lacking and one is a very high-profile and affluent city in the Los Angeles area that ends in *Hills*.

But this book won't leave the reader with naught on ROM cost modeling. ROM cost modeling is approached very much like the Needs Identification process using the OSI model. The most basic and immediately useable method, of course, is to use a spreadsheet program and start at the bottom of the OSI model and move up.

ROM cost modeling must have a starting point, expanded through definition of each cost component, and then be taken to the Nh degree to achieve what is known as "outside budgeting." Outside budgeting is a method to ensure that estimates are high instead of low. It is always better to have high-budget estimates than low ones. However, they shouldn't be so high as to not provide an accurate basis for the feasibility study. If ROM estimates are not based on actual cost modeling methods, the ROM cost model may derail the whole project when it comes to the feasibility study.

Each ROM estimate must start with the primary components. For instance in the Wi-Fi Implementation scenario (table 3.1), the object equipment, primarily the network and wireless equipment is a fine starting point.

**Table 3.1  Scenario One—Wi-Fi Implementation: Systems Recommendations**

| | |
|---|---|
| Objective | Implement Wi-Fi throughout all sites to support 1:1 computing. |
| Scope | Wi-Fi which may include additional switches, cabling, antennae, and control systems. |
| Scale | All sites, with enough bandwidth to support every student one device (1:1). |
| Business Need | All online curriculum must be accessible to each student using a mobile device. |
| System Need | All sites require wireless network infrastructure, equipment, and control software to support student device mobility. |
| Technical Needs | 1. Structured Cabling<br>  a. New main distribution frame (MDF) and intermediate distribution frame (IDF) facilities upgrades capable of supporting new structured cabling and associated power, racks, and enclosures.<br>  b. New MDF and IDF power upgrades<br>    i. May require new survey, transformers, and ducting<br>  c. New pathways, trenching, and conduit installation between MDF and IDF closets.<br>  d. New fiber-optic backbone cabling (OM4)<br>  e. New copper-horizontal cabling (Cat6)<br>2. Network Equipment (10 Gbps)<br>  a. Core switches<br>  b. Edge switches<br>  c. VoIP phones<br>3. Wi-Fi Equipment<br>  a. Wireless Controllers<br>  b. Wireless Control Systems (Servers and Management suite)<br>  c. Wireless Access Points (WAPs). |
| Systems Recommendations | Wireless Network System includes:<br>• Facilities Construction<br>  ○ MDF/IDF construction<br>  ○ Trenching, Pathways, Conduit<br>• Structured Cabling Installation<br>  ○ Fiber-Optic Backbone<br>  ○ Copper-Horizontal Cabling<br>• Network Equipment<br>• Wi-Fi Equipment |

The cost components detailed in the Systems Recommendations will become the basis for creating the ROM estimate.

Figure 3.2 shows how the planner can use the OSI model to identify the granular components of a complex IT environment.

A simple spreadsheet allocating hardware to locations is likely the best way to start building the ROM estimate for the Wi-Fi project. The planner may decide to use a site plan of each building or location and use that to develop

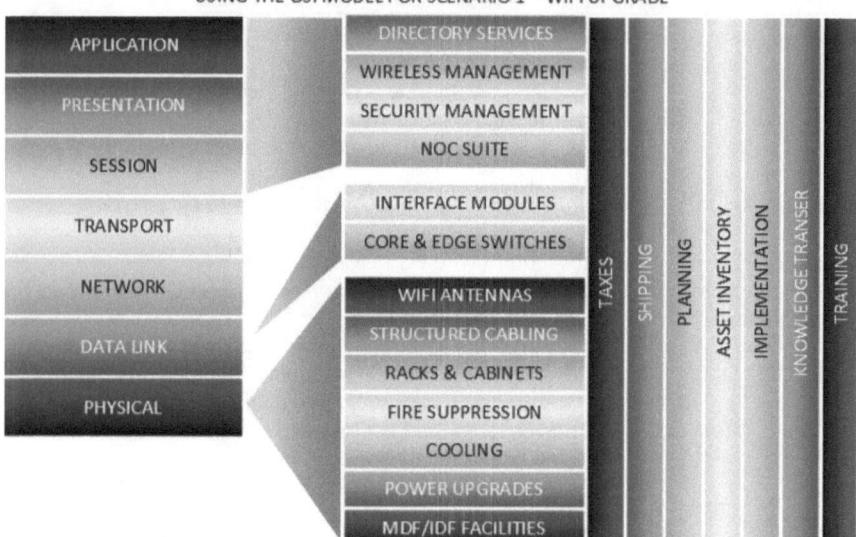

Figure 3.2  Wi-Fi ROM Cost Model.

a plan for the location of wireless antennae and the associated cabling. From this graphic model, the planner then can count the number of locations and cables and set them up on the spreadsheet.

Each individual site may require a full spreadsheet table (rows and columns) so that multiple spreadsheets will be required to create the full cost model. This might be referred to as a 3-dimensional (3D) cost model, and can leverage many of the current spreadsheet and 3D modeling tools like arrays, database features, and pivot tables.

As can be seen by looking at the elements of the Systems Recommendations, each area or trade, will require intimate knowledge of the aspects of estimating.

The main distribution frame (MDF) and intermediate distribution frame (IDF) locations must be identified and assessed for capacity, power, and environment. This assessment will require a facilities person for structural and cooling, and a power person for high voltage and grounding. Will these locations require extra security or monitoring? What about fire suppression?

For instance, estimating the construction costs of MDF upgrades, trenching, and conduit installation would be best done by a general contractor. Even the in-house facilities director will likely have to go to an outside contractor for this type of work.

The structured cabling would be best estimated by a low-voltage cabling contractor, as with the networking and Wi-Fi equipment best estimated by a system integrator.

In all these cases, the "materials" (hardware, software, and miscellaneous) would be one component, with an installation labor component corresponding with each. It is never enough to use just the equipment without adding installation labor. And that's just for the facilities upgrades. With networking equipment there is also planning, staging, pre-configuration, asset inventory tagging, and secondary deployment and staging, all before installation. Which may also beg the question about the removal and disposal of old equipment (oops, that's another huge can of worms that will be discussed later).

In order to best solve complex cost models, start with a unit cost basis for each cost element. Standard unit costs for construction upgrades will be significantly affected by the need for architectural services. For instance, in upgrading an existing room for additional cooling, an allocation for additional power would also be logical, as well as additional estimates and contingency for unexpected construction needs. But if a new facility is being built from the ground up, square-foot estimating standards along with architectural services could easily double or triple the cost estimates. Beware, when including construction costs in ROM estimates. They must be qualified and escalated over time.

Past construction projects can provide the basis for estimating future projects by measuring their similarity and time lapsed, and developing an outside estimate to correspond with the unit costing. Don't forget to include the architect, construction management and/or developer fees, and permits that may be associated with the construction. For instance, if it cost $10,000 to upgrade power and cooling to one MDF in the past, this number, escalated for time lapsed (inflation) could be the basis for the estimates for similar upgrades to all other IDFs.

Similarly, if the low-voltage duct back for a small elementary school cost $1,000,000 ten years ago, then this number can form the basis for a new standard estimate subject to escalation. It is always advisable to bring in experts in the trade for aid in estimating.

Structured cabling can be estimated in various ways. For fiber-optic backbone, it is typical to know from scaled plans, the approximate length of each run. However, material cost of fiber-optic cabling is only a small element in the cost estimate. There are a huge assortment of additional materials like racks, terminations, cable managers, innerduct, and so on. There is also labor associated with the installation of each cable at each end, as well as fiber termination expertise for each strand on each end. That's why using 12-strand fiber cabling costs so much more than installing 6-strand cabling, even though they are pulling the same length and number of cables, the number of fiber terminations to be polished, terminated, and racked is double.

For copper-horizontal cabling, it is best to assume the maximum length of cabling (100 meters per run) and then develop a unit cost per drop (or dual drop). Build the materials and standard termination and installation labor into each drop. Of course, this unit cost may not account for efficiencies of scope or scale but keep in mind, it is better to be high at this phase than to miss something significant and estimate too low. Don't let the school's in-house installer do the estimate. He typically knows things and does things differently than a licensed contractor would. Unless he's recently put in a similar project out to bid, his estimate would need to be compared to another method in order to validate it.

This is an important exercise when developing and revising cost model estimates. Sometimes it is advisable to use two or even three different estimating methods for a cost model. Maybe a square foot, construction estimate, and a unit cost per drop plus labor estimate are compared to a recent similar construction project. Compare the three and take the highest one to be on the outside of the cost model.

The trickiest part may be proposing and estimating new copper-horizontal network drops. If the existing drops are at least Cat5e, there should be no reason to replace these. But if not, then should new cables be installed to replace EACH existing drop? Should a standard be developed for each location? These types of assumptions will become a major cost factor in any ROM that includes structured cabling.

Schools are their own breed of copper networks. Instead of deciding on the number of locations, they require standards for each classroom and non-classroom area. For instance, most schools will install at least two network drops on each wall, and then two in the ceiling for Wireless Access Points (WAPs). But 10 Cat6 drops in each classroom can easily blow a budget. Especially when everything is going wireless. Some might question why any wall drops are required if everything is going wireless? Only desktop computers, network printers, and Internet Protocol (IP) telephones should be cabled anymore because these devices are optimized for a wired connection.

Network equipment is relatively easy to estimate. The planner can start with a hardware Bill of Materials (BOM) and include taxes and shipping. Using the manufacturer's list pricing is a good technique for outside budgeting since a pretty significant discount from list can usually be attained in the procurement process. If not, then the organization is not getting the best value. The planner should be sure to include the first year (at least) of maintenance and support for the equipment.

If the sample BOM is not a real-one from a previous order, then the planner takes the risk of missing major cost elements such as miscellaneous cables or components, special licensing upgrades, software configurations, or redundant power supplies. To mitigate this, the planner should get help from a real customer service representative that can get their hands on real pricing and configuration tools. The planner should be well aware that obtaining free help from a system integrator could cause conflicts of interest problems with big procurements—if that system integrator wants to bid on the project later. The planner is advised to follow state contracting and procurement guidelines to be safe.

Cost models should also account for recurring costs and/or maintenance agreements and licenses. Although these costs may not affect the system design, capturing all known costs is critical to cost modeling and an important consideration for the feasibility study and the Chief Financial Officer.

A ROM estimate developed in the Recommendations phase may be designated ROM1, because as the solution becomes more detailed and investigated, the cost model will be more refined and accurate (table 3.2).

A quick review of the Needs Analysis illustrates that the first step defined—Systems Needs to Recommendations—New SIS system and associated requirements—is a huge step. That means in moving from Analysis to Recommendations, the planner had to at the very minimum,

1. Define the system requirements
2. Survey all systems available that support these requirements
    a. Once again, alternative technologies comparison may be required to provide in-depth technical and cost comparisons.
3. Compare the systems features and pricing
4. Test and/or validate the systems
5. Make a recommendation.

In figure 3.3, one will recognize the familiar Wi-Fi infrastructure needed to provide mobility to the SIS project, but also note the mobile SIS Apps, the core SIS Application, its associated Structured Query Language (SQL) Database Platform, and the Operating System (OS) environment these platforms are running on.

In addition, at the lower levels are detailed infrastructure required including the data center equipment supporting the new SIS applications: archive, storage, fabric, and compute platforms all needing to be identified, and modeled into the ROM.

For a large-scale Student Information System (SIS), this can easily be the largest part of the project. The salient point being, beyond detailing the process of system selection, the planner takes on full responsibility to perform it and make the recommendation.

## Planner Perspectives

The planner must be very careful of the release of early budget information. The early estimates coming into ROM1 may be so inaccurate that sharing of this information with anyone could throw the process into an unnecessary tailspin. When meeting with stakeholders and department heads regarding

**Table 3.2  Scenario Two—Student Information System (SIS) Selection: Systems Recommendations**

| | |
|---|---|
| Objectives | 1. Identify and implement new SIS system<br>2. Upgrade network and computing infrastructure to support online SIS access and mobility. |
| Scope | 1. SIS Selection<br>2. Network Infrastructure and Wireless Saturation |
| Scale | 1. All students<br>2. All sites |
| Business Needs | 1. The district must have access to all student information to comply with federal and state reporting, testing as well as all relevant personal and academic data.<br>2. The district network must support robust wired and wireless computing in order to access the SIS. |
| Systems Needs | 1. The district requires a SIS that addresses all the Business Needs.<br>2. The district network system requires additional infrastructure, equipment, and software to support SIS application performance and mobility. |
| Technical Needs | 1. New SIS system—System Selection Process. Required Feature Set<br>2. Structured Cabling<br>   a. New main distribution frame (MDF) and intermediate distribution frame (IDF) facilities upgrades capable of supporting new structured cabling and associated power, racks, and enclosures.<br>   b. New MDF and IDF power upgrades<br>      i. May require new survey, transformers, and ducting<br>   c. New pathways, trenching, and conduit installation between MDF and IDF closets.<br>   d. New fiber-optic backbone cabling (OM4)<br>   e. New copper-horizontal cabling (Cat6)<br>3. Network Equipment (10 Gbps)<br>   a. Core switches<br>   b. Edge switches<br>   c. VoIP phones<br>4. Wi-Fi Equipment<br>   a. Wireless Controllers<br>   b. Wireless Control Systems (Servers and Management suite)<br>   c. Wireless Access Points (WAPs). |
| Systems Recommendations | New SIS system<br>• SIS Mobile Apps<br>• SIS Application Software License<br>• System Database Platform<br>• System Operating System Platform<br>• Compute System<br>• SAN Fabric<br>• Storage Network |

## Recommendations

- Archive System

Wireless Network System includes:
- Facilities Construction
  - MDF/IDF construction
  - Trenching, Pathways, Conduit
- Structured Cabling Installation
  - Fiber-Optic Backbone
  - Copper-Horizontal Cabling
- Network Equipment
- Wi-Fi Equipment

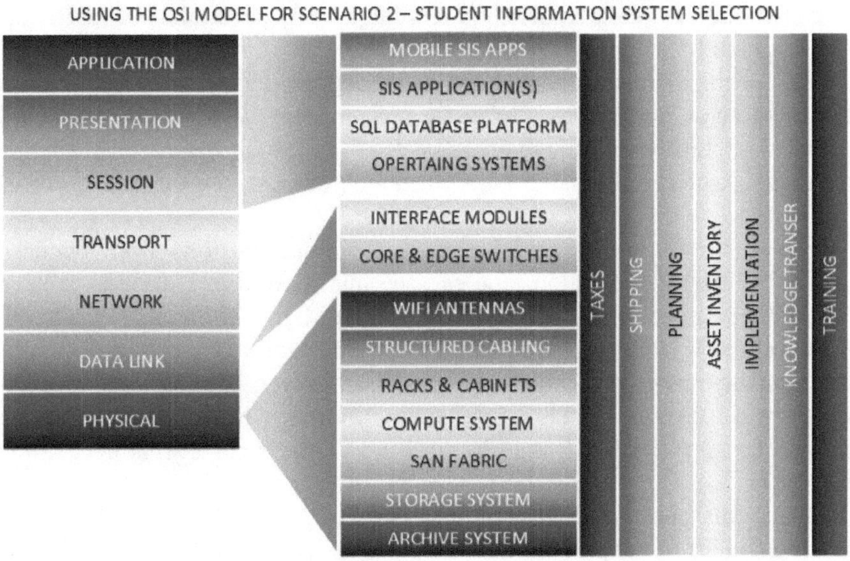

USING THE OSI MODEL FOR SCENARIO 2 – STUDENT INFORMATION SYSTEM SELECTION

| OSI Layer | Component | |
|---|---|---|
| APPLICATION | MOBILE SIS APPS | |
| | SIS APPLICATION(S) | |
| PRESENTATION | SQL DATABASE PLATFORM | |
| SESSION | OPERATING SYSTEMS | |
| TRANSPORT | INTERFACE MODULES | |
| | CORE & EDGE SWITCHES | |
| NETWORK | WIFI ANTENNAS | |
| DATA LINK | STRUCTURED CABLING | |
| | RACKS & CABINETS | |
| PHYSICAL | COMPUTE SYSTEM | |
| | SAN FABRIC | |
| | STORAGE SYSTEM | |
| | ARCHIVE SYSTEM | |

Additional columns: TAXES, SHIPPING, PLANNING, ASSET INVENTORY, IMPLEMENTATION, KNOWLEDGE TRANSFER, TRAINING

**Figure 3.3  SIS Selection ROM Cost Model.**

ROM budget development, it is wise to limit the discussion to the scope of the stakeholder's involvement. They may not and should not have intimate understanding of budget capacity and constraints outside their realm of influence. They are likely to editorialize on what can be afforded and what can be purchased, but this guidance may be flawed or biased.

The planner should focus on gathering all relevant comments and information and then assemble the ROM separately, sharing only limited amounts of information with certain stakeholders in an attempt to create an unbiased estimate, which is required for the Blue Sky design approach. Once again, the planner is cautioned about the appearance that they are withholding information.

# Chapter Three

## TECHNICAL RECOMMENDATIONS

Once the planner has developed the Systems Recommendations, it begins to become very clear what the Technical Recommendations will look like. Technical Recommendations should be detailed and specific enough to use as Performance Requirements for a bid document. Remember that performance requirements define how a system should perform, not necessarily what hardware, software, and services to purchase.

Performance requirements are used to define the requirements of systems that might compete against each other without specifying manufacturer's names or hardware products. And again, since this is still the Blue Sky planning methodology, the planner should not inject any constraints or limitations to the system.

The Technical Recommendations must address every component of the Systems Recommendations. For instance Scenario One—Wi-Fi, will require technical specifications for every aspect of the system based on their procurements. Once again, using the OSI model, one can see the specifications required (see table 3.3).

From this example of the Technical Recommendations from Scenario One—Wi-Fi implementation, one can see that it would be quite expansive. Developing the technical specifications for the MDF/IDF rooms alone would be a multipage document referencing current state and local code regarding construction of data center type facilities, power, cooling, and fire. And procuring the construction is a completely different type of procurement than the equipment purchase. It may be a Public Works contract that needs to be executed.

It is at this point in the planning process that the planner will begin to develop an idea of the project's overall complexity. And although the plan has still not been quantified or qualified through the feasibility study, the planner would have a pretty good idea of the separate procurements and steps that would be required to complete the project. For instance, it is easy to recognize that all the MDF/IDF construction must be completed before any of the structured cabling can begin.

The IT director might need significant support from the Facilities department, the Engineering department, and the Maintenance and Operations departments for these subprojects, yet they will be in the critical path for the strategic initiatives. What is the impact of this statement?

If the Facilities director doesn't have the same priorities as this project requires, and he is responsible for upgrading the MDF and IDF facilities, then any delay in these construction projects will delay all the subsequent project dependent on the MDF/IDF infrastructure (table 3.4).

**Table 3.3  Scenario One—Wi-Fi Implementation: Technical Recommendations**

| | |
|---|---|
| Objective | Implement Wi-Fi throughout all sites to support 1:1 computing. |
| Scope | Wi-Fi which may include additional switches, cabling, antennae, and control systems. |
| Scale | All sites, with enough bandwidth to support every student one device (1:1). |
| Business Need | All online curriculum must be accessible to each student using a mobile device. |
| System Need | All sites require wireless network infrastructure, equipment, and control software to support student device mobility. |
| Technical Needs | 1. Structured Cabling<br>  a. New main distribution frame (MDF) and intermediate distribution frame (IDF) facilities upgrades capable of supporting new structured cabling and associated power, racks, and enclosures.<br>  b. New MDF and IDF power upgrades<br>    i. May require new survey, transformers, and ducting<br>  c. New pathways, trenching, and conduit installation between MDF and IDF closets.<br>  d. New fiber-optic backbone cabling (OM4)<br>  e. New copper-horizontal cabling (Cat6)<br>2. Network Equipment (10 Gbps)<br>  a. Core switches<br>  b. Edge switches<br>  c. VoIP phones<br>3. Wi-Fi Equipment<br>  a. Wireless Controllers<br>  b. Wireless Control Systems (Servers and Management suite)<br>  c. Wireless Access Points (WAPs). |
| Systems Recommendation | Wireless Network System includes:<br>• Facilities Construction<br>  ○ MDF/IDF Construction<br>  ○ Trenching, Pathways, Conduit<br>• Structured Cabling Installation<br>  ○ Fiber-Optic Backbone<br>  ○ Copper-Horizontal Cabling<br>• Network Equipment<br>• Wi-Fi Equipment |
| Technical Recommendations | 1. MDF/IDF Rooms<br>  a. Power Requirements<br>  b. Rack and Enclosures<br>  c. Cooling<br>  d. Fire Suppression |

(continued)

**Table 3.3** (continued)

|  |  |
|---|---|
| | 2. Structured Cabling<br>   a. Fiber-Optic Backbone Cabling<br>      i. Terminations<br>      ii. Routing<br>      iii. Testing<br>   b. Copper-Horizontal Cabling<br>      i. Terminations<br>      ii. Routing/Installation<br>      iii. Testing<br>3. Network Equipment (10 Gbps)<br>   a. Core Switch<br>   b. Edge Switch<br>4. Wireless Equipment<br>   a. Wireless Control and Management<br>   b. Wireless Antennae |

**Table 3.4** Scenario Two—Student Information System (SIS) Selection: Technical Recommendations

| | |
|---|---|
| Objectives | 1. Identify and implement new SIS system<br>2. Upgrade network and computing infrastructure to support online SIS access and mobility. |
| Scope | 1. SIS Selection<br>2. Network Infrastructure and Wireless Saturation |
| Scale | 1. All students<br>2. All sites |
| Business Needs | 1. The district must have access to all student information to comply with federal and state reporting, testing as well as all relevant personal and academic data.<br>2. The district network must support robust wired and wireless computing in order to access the SIS. |
| Systems Needs | 1. The district requires a Student Information System that addresses all the Business Needs.<br>2. The district network system requires additional infrastructure, equipment and software to support SIS application performance and mobility. |
| Technical Needs | 1. New SIS System—System Selection Processa. Required Feature Set<br>2. Structured Cabling<br>   a. New main distribution frame (MDF) and intermediate distribution frame (IDF) facilities upgrades capable of supporting new structured cabling and associated power, racks, and enclosures.<br>   b. New MDF and IDF power upgrades<br>      i. May require new survey, transformers, and ducting<br>   c. New pathways, trenching and conduit installation between MDF and IDF closets. |

| | |
|---|---|
| | d. New Fiber-Optic Backbone Cabling (OM4) |
| | e. New Copper-Horizontal Cabling (Cat6) |
| | 3. Network Equipment (10 Gbps) |
| |    a. Core switches |
| |    b. Edge switches |
| |    c. VoIP phones |
| | 4. Wi-Fi Equipment |
| |    a. Wireless Controllers |
| |    b. Wireless Control Systems (Servers and Management suite) |
| |    c. Wireless Access Points (WAPs). |
| Systems Recommendations | New SIS System<br>• System Hardware platform<br>• System OS platform<br>• System DB platform<br>• System License<br>Wireless Network System includes:<br>• Facilities Construction<br>   ○ MDF/IDF Construction<br>   ○ Trenching, Pathways, Conduit<br>• Structured Cabling Installation<br>   ○ Fiber-Optic Backbone<br>   ○ Copper-Horizontal Cabling<br>• Network Equipment<br>• Wi-Fi Equipment |
| Technical Recommendations | Hardware Platform Requirements<br>Operating System Requirements<br>Database Platform Requirements<br>Software and Licensing Requirements<br>Wi-Fi System—See Scenario One—Wi-Fi |

In Scenario Two—SIS Selection, it is detailed that all the network infrastructure components required to support the fully functional SIS system (which specifically requires mobility = Wi-Fi) includes the entire Scenario One—Wi-Fi scope as a subproject. At this point, it might become glaringly clear to the planner that these are really two separate projects, even if they are being funded by the same budget and one is dependent on the other.

Upon completion of the Recommendations phase, the ROM cost model should be fairly well detailed. By this time, ROM1 or possibly developing ROM2 should be completed. The reader might be wondering, what is the point of designating ROM1 and ROM2 and so on. Isn't there just one ROM? Well yes and no. It is always a good practice to maintain the original ROM to see: (1) that subsequent ROMs are becoming more accurate, and (2) the original ROM is used to compare initial assumptions and estimating methods.

For instance, in ROM1, a general MDF/IDF construction estimate might have been used based on a square foot calculation. But in ROM2, a comparative construction project might have been used to better-estimate the construction and each of the trade areas.

**Planner Perspectives**

Once again, the planner might find ROM2 estimates to be higher for whatever reasons, so the outside budgeting method must be held intact to keep the number from going upside-down. The planner might have been very wise not to share the ROM1 estimate with anyone.

The last thing a successful plan needs, is to have a ROM cost model estimate that is too low and restricts the feasibility study, or that is too high and the discussion becomes misinformed.

When it comes to the time to do the feasibility study, an official ROM will need to be referenced. Whether this is ROM1 or ROM2 may not need to be publicized to anyone. However, the ROM used for the feasibility study will become the official "ROM1."

## PRELIMINARY DESIGN

The output from the Recommendations phase and based on the design direction is the preliminary design. This design should consist of the following items:

- Logical Design Diagram
- Design Narrative
- ROM1
- Preliminary Phasing.

The proposed logical design diagram is the result of the GAP analysis. It is the proposed solution set that has been developing through the Needs Identification and Needs Analysis phases. Once the System Recommendations and Technical Recommendations have been developed, the proposed design diagram must once again be revised to illustrate the direction of the Preliminary Recommendations. This design is one step more detailed than the proposed design developed for the GAP analysis. The GAP analysis can only be as detailed as the business systems that would support the objectives. This new preliminary design should clearly detail systems and technologies to provide the feasibility study and stakeholders with a coherent, well-thought-out design proposal. The important point to note at this time is, this is still the Blue Sky solution being presented. Why? Because if the Blue Sky proposal doesn't fulfill all the program objectives, there is no hope that a lesser plan could do so. And up until this point, there has been no research or discovery about the fiscal situation that could prematurely influence or constrain cost.

The design narrative is the necessary prose that accompanies the logical design. Although a picture is worth a thousand words, a design diagram without a design narrative is left open to all the questions of the picture viewer and all their worldly lack of knowledge.

## CHAPTER THREE ESSENTIALS

1. The inputs of the Recommendations phase are the Systems Needs and Technical Needs from the Needs Analysis process.
2. This is the first phase that focuses on Solutions as opposed to Needs.
3. The Blue Sky approach is used to develop a design that is sure to address all the objectives and not limited by cost.
4. If the Blue Sky approach doesn't address all the objectives, then the plan will likely fall short, in the eyes of some.
5. The Systems Recommendations and Technical Recommendations will provide the basis for the design direction.
6. In overly complex plans, an Alternative Technologies study may be warranted.
7. The design direction provides the basis for the Preliminary Recommendations and the first of a series of Rough Order Magnitude cost estimates.

*Chapter Four*

# Feasibility Study

Feasibility is the phase of the planning process where reality is applied to the Blue Sky solution set (figure 4.1). In an effort to ensure a plan developed is a plan executed, the feasibility study is where the "rubber meets the road." If there is no real money available, what is the point of developing a plan? The only way to develop a plan that can be executed is that the funding must be available to execute the plan. No money, no point. In fact, it makes sense to ask, who's paying the bill for the time already spent?

The feasibility study may be the most difficult part of the plan to get scheduled and to make happen, and it may take a lot of time to get it going. So the expectation must be set very early-on in the process, that there will be a "meeting" with the Chief Financial Officer (CFO) to discuss the availability of funding.

In fact, if the planner cannot rise beyond the level of the IT director to validate available funding, then the planning may all be for naught. Of course, there is a possibility that the IT director has full knowledge and authority over funding, but this is not usually the case.

That doesn't mean that every IT endeavor doesn't need a plan if there isn't a dedicated budget. It is typical that in order to "ask for money," there must be a detailed plan. However, there are instances where an IT director would develop an implementation plan that doesn't require a budget—but that really means that it doesn't require an *additional* budget, because there is obviously a budget for their department already. The director might develop a plan based on current staff, resources, and time, simply by reallocating resources and redefining priorities.

Feasibility within the MAPIT™ framework is measured in two contexts: Physical and Fiscal.

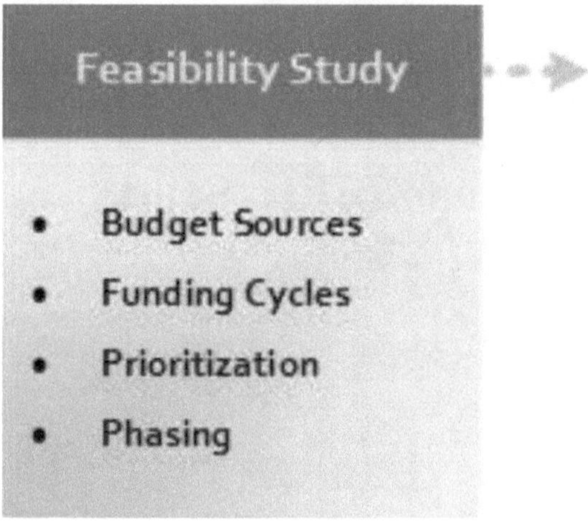

**Figure 4.1** Feasibility Study.

Physical may also be referred to as "practical." Fiscal feasibility is the main component for MAPIT™. Unless specifically mentioned in the Recommendations, a physical feasibility study may not be necessary. For instance, in both scenarios we've been studying, there are likely no physical constraints to those two particular circumstances. So what would be a physical feasibility study?

If the objectives called for a new data center room, and there is no physical space to accommodate new construction, then this new data center construction would be not physically feasible. But let's consider the implications of such an outcome. If the Business Needs require a dedicated or upgraded data center facility, and the feasibility study deems this physically not feasible, that would immediately stop the project. The only way for this project to continue would be for the planner to convince the stakeholders that this data center is not a key objective of the project and that other accommodations would have to be accepted in order for this project to be considered a success.

The feasibility study is also a great indicator of the level of visibility and acceptance of the project up to this point. Typically, 95 percent of the discovery and early Needs Analysis phases requires interaction with the IT staff and department heads. Kick-off meetings and status update meetings may include higher-level stakeholders. However, the feasibility study must be performed in a very intimate setting with the financial authority of the organization. This may be a CFO, Business Officer, or Accountant, either way, this is not a typical IT type person. For further discussions, this all-knowing financial person will be referred to as the CFO.

Before delving into how to conduct the feasibility study and interview, it is important to understand some realities of the fiscal environment in public and private schools. IT budgeting is not a standardized practice although it certainly should be. In fact, it is still very common to walk into a small- to medium-sized school or district and find there is no designated IT budget. Line items for personnel, software licenses, and telecommunications services may be the extent of it. And this is where the planning process really hits the Go or No-Go milestone. It is important to remember that the budget in development, up until this point, is a Blue Sky budget.

If the Chief Business Official (CBO) has no warning or understanding of the planning process he may be totally unprepared for this process.

In this sense the planner may be walking into an ambush for this meeting. How so? The reader may ask. Typically, the CFO or CBO or accountant will know about the planning project (since he probably had to sign off on the purchase order). However, once the kick-off meetings are held and the project team goes into discovery mode, the CBO may not hear about it from the team for weeks. Unless this person continues to be on the key communications updates, he may not be up-to-date on the project.

So, the planner is best advised to schedule this meeting well ahead of time and provide a clear agenda that presents the expectation of a discussion of technology-budget availability. The candor of this meeting will be the litmus test of the entire project success. If significant information about funding and its availability are withheld from the planner, major project disruption or a catastrophic project end may be triggered.

For example, if the CFO held back the fact that an additional 50 percent of funding might be available (that would mean an additional $500,000 in a $1,000,000 budget) the planner might be forced to limit the scope, scale, or priority of projects to a greater extent than might be possible with the extra funding. Or worse, if the CFO did not disclose that some unrelated budgetary event could occur to impact the stated amount of funding, the planner could propose and begin executing a plan, but run out of funding in the middle of the project.

Table 4.1 shows a sample feasibility study meeting agenda.

## BUDGET SOURCES

In a fiscally complex environment, the discussion of the availability of funds can be a sensitive one. The planner is best advised to ask questions straight up and directly, and shouldn't be surprised to be met with deflection and obfuscation. The planner's quandary is his need to know some things about the fiscal environment controlled by the CFO, but there are many things in his realm

Table 4.1  Sample Feasibility Study Meeting Agenda

| Phase Four | Feasibility Study |
|---|---|
| Agenda | Planning Methodology Review |
| | GAP analysis |
| | Preliminary Recommendations |
| | Rough Order Magnitude (ROM) budget |
| Objectives | Budget sources |
| | Funding cycle |
| | Prioritization |
| | Phasing |
| | Rescoping Rescaling |

that the planner doesn't need to know. Simply asking about funding sources can be too much to ask for. Never fear, however, as he should wrap himself in the flag of the stated objectives, scope, time, and budget. He can't be faulted for asking, but he must also be prepared to not get an answer. Suffice to say, the CFO may only tell the planner what he needs to know, but that should be enough. The planner should know when he's got all he's going to get, and be satisfied. The risk being that the CFO did not divulge all the possible funding available, and thereby has handicapped the planning project. But there is no recourse for the planner at this point.

Budget sources are important because different piles of money may have different spending prerequisites—they may not be discretionary, meaning that they must be spent for a certain type of equipment or services. They may not be able to be used for services or maintenance contracts. Although the actual source of the money may be immaterial and not disclosed to the planner, the more information that can be obtained and gleaned, the better the planner is equipped to complete the planning project.

So ultimately, the budget source is less important than the budget capacity—if the CBO gives an assurance that $1,000,000.00 WILL BE available, then that will just have to do.

## FUNDING CYCLES

The funding cycles are specific to the timing of the availability of funds. They may be multiyear, one-time, or recurring. Oftentimes, these budgets are tied to fiscal-year cycles or bond sales. Therefore, implementations are organized into phases by priority.

By using a GANTT chart or project management software like MS Project, the planner can begin to lay out the amount of dollars and time-frame that the monies become available.

Ultimately, the funding allocations will be detailed by project with their associated costs. These will be reflected in the final budget as well (ROM3).

## PRIORITIZATION

Prioritization is the ordering or sequencing of projects and/or events to facilitate completion of the overall project. Many projects need not be sequential, meaning that certain projects or subprojects can begin and be executed simultaneously. It usually comes down to budget. The more available the budget, the faster the things can happen. Things can be managed to occur simultaneously so that a twenty-four-month plan could become a twelve-month plan if the funding is available.

Oftentimes in the early engagement and proposal process, an expectation of plan duration should be stated. Is this a six-month plan, or a three-year plan? One might note that a three-year plan should be strategic, while a six-month plan would be tactical and implementation focused. Technology plans beyond five years make less sense and are less specific.

The planner must be cognizant of the perception of the expenditures by the stakeholders and the community at large, especially when bond or tax dollars are being spent. For instance, if the planner only prioritizes initiatives by infrastructure need, then he might not plan any user-impacting expenditures until the later phases. But the user-impacting expenditures may be of more priority to the users and stakeholders. As an example, the planner might think the priority is to spend all the year-one funding on infrastructure, however, the user-base might be looking for new computers in year-one. Whose requirement is more important?

This becomes the ultimate balancing act. Unless leadership accepts that infrastructure must come first before any user-impacting technologies (such as devices), then the planner's conundrum is solved. It is always best to complete infrastructure upgrades before deploying end-user devices, but the need to deploy some devices (to key stakeholders) may be a driving factor of some very important users, power users, or board members. And these preferences and priorities should have been identified in the discovery process (but not necessarily detailed in the narratives or documentation).

It is not uncommon or unwise to use the technology department and staff as "guinea pigs" to test out new technologies and devices before rolling them out to the general user base.

One can also see, how the funding cycle may restrict how much of each project can be done initially. For instance if the Data Center construction is a Phase One component, but not enough funding is available in phase one to complete it, then the planner should be able to begin initial construction on the Data Center project while also delivering other near-term projects so that when the funding comes available to complete the data center, the other infrastructure items that will leverage it will already be in operation.

## Planner Perspectives

This is the balancing act of Prioritization and Phasing. And it is best not developed in a vacuum. These types of potentially controversial decision points should be done with as many high-profile participants and leadership in support. That way, when the questions are asked, the leaders and stakeholders who advocated these details and decisions will be there to carry the debate. Or at the minimum, the planner can pronounce, "this decision was made by these people at this meeting on this date."

It is easy for the planner to get caught up in the details of the prioritization but there is no need for any type of personal or emotional investment in the planning process. It is the client's environment and program. If they want something in a particular way, then it's the planner's job to deliver it—editorial opinions notwithstanding. For the most part, the planner should do what he's told. Just keep a historical record of the interactions and communications.

## PHASING

Phasing is the sequencing of procurements and implementations according to priorities and funding. By this point in the planning process, the planner should begin utilizing some type of resource/project planning tool to begin to lay out the technology initiatives, in order to develop a sense for the project plan duration.

The planner must keep in mind that public works construction and larger procurements need more planning, take more time, and may require formalized contracting and procurement strategies. Although not as common in private sector companies, formal bid processes and Requests for Proposals (RFPs) are extremely common and are often required for procurements above $45,000 in public sector agencies.

Also, many states and governments require formal and informal bidding processes, and while the use of state contracts, prenegotiated contracts, and procurement schedules are common practice, it should be understood that the ONLY way to ensure the lowest price is by formal competitive bidding. Although contractors and system integrators will give assurances that the district is getting the "street price," if they aren't in a competitive situation, there is no way they are giving their best possible price. There's just no need.

The salient point for this phasing discussion is that the more parties involved (construction), or the more money involved, the longer it takes to

**Table 4.2  Sample Project Duration Timelines**

| Org Type | Work Type | Threshold | Vehicle | Duration (weeks) |
|---|---|---|---|---|
| School or School District | Construction | <$45,000 | Purchase order | 2–8 |
| | | >$45,000 | Contract | 4–12 |
| | | >$200,000 | RFP/Contract | 6–24 |
| | Equipment | <$45,000 | Purchase order | 2–4 |
| | | >$45,000 | Informal bid | 2–8 |
| | | >$85,000 | Formal bid/RFP | 8–16 |

procure. The following table 4.2 shows example timelines for project durations in public and private sector organizations. These estimated time frames are for procurement times—not inclusive of inventory, shipping, and delivery times which may also vary based on equipment type, scope, and scale.

In the public sector (particularly in California) state contracting code requires Division 27—Communications Systems and specific RFP guidelines to support formal bidding processes. Construction may also require additional state architect's approvals such as the Department of General Services and Division of State Architects (DSA) approval which also provides special review for Schools, Classrooms, and all instructional venues. These submission and approval processes can easily last six months to one year from the Architect's Construction Documents to actual ground breaking.

## FINAL RECOMMENDATIONS

The final recommendations are not a separate report. They are the output of the feasibility study. The reason that this doesn't have to be a formal report separate from the other documents is that the actual strategic plan and subordinate Implementation Plans are the direct evolution and result of the final recommendations. So the planner can skip this additional document within the document and move directly to development of the strategic plan, which will consist of evolutions of the Proposed Technical Architecture, Final Recommendations, and ROM Budget estimates. The only thing missing at this point is the graphical depiction of this "strategy" and the compiled report.

## CHAPTER FOUR ESSENTIALS

1. The inputs coming from the Recommendations include the Preliminary Design and the first (published) ROM cost model.

2. The feasibility study should be the first time the planner takes cost and cost constraints into consideration.
3. The planner should establish the importance of meeting with the CBO and the agenda well in advance.
4. The CBO may not be willing to share some budget information. The planner must establish the need for the availability of funds and any restrictions on the monies.
5. The outputs are the Final Recommendations and revised ROM, which will become the inputs for the Strategic and Implementation Plans.

*Chapter Five*

# Design and Implementation

This chapter is the point of this book—the meat on the bones, the fruit of the labor, the deliverable. It's odd to note that these deliverables are nothing but ideas, thought through, researched, planned, budgeted, and sequenced (figure 5.1). Still there is no Data Center, Structured Cabling, Wi-Fi, or devices. Nothing has been built and no money expended (except those dollars expended to develop the strategy and plans).

So what has been accomplished when all this discovery, analysis, and design is complete? The Education Technology Strategy and Implementation Plans can be considered marching orders—a PLAN—an actionable set of tasks and activities. Armed with this plan a project manager can procure, implement, and deploy. These deliverables will become the inputs to the MAPIT™ Project Management Core and Support processes which are the processes that support execution.

Each of the deliverables, along with the documents developed up through this point (see all items in the MAPIT™ Planning processes in figure 5.2) will combine to form the Technology Strategic Plan Report.

## THE STRATEGIC PLAN

It has been repeated more than once in this book regarding the Logical Design, a picture is worth a thousand words. And it is true. One of the most effective ways to lead an audience through a complex discussion is by using visual diagrams that correlate and support ideas, plans, and strategies.

However, key diagrams and graphics are more than just boxes, colors, and gradients. The words in the boxes must be meaningful and specific to its audience. For instance, the strategy diagram in figure 5.3 is an actual diagram

70                              *Chapter Five*

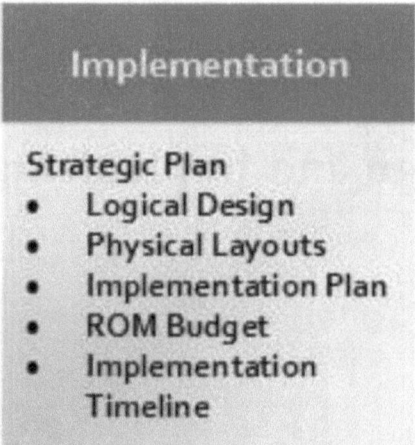

Figure 5.1   Implementation.

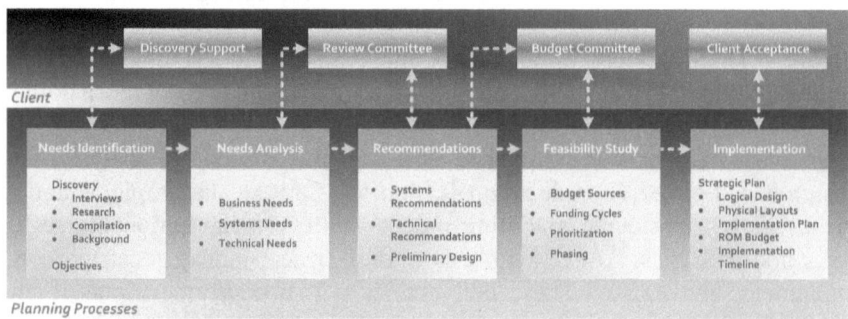

Figure 5.2   Planning Process Deliverables.

from a recent project. The directional arrows illustrate movement from left to right.

The labels at the bottom communicate the movement from Strategic Initiatives to Technology Initiatives which in turn identify Tactical Plans (figure 5.3). The titles in the Strategic Initiatives are all familiar to the audience because they were cherry-picked from the organization's formal written objectives and strategic business plans—for example, a school district's Board Goals and LCAP Goals.

Using a visual tool to relate to known business or educational strategies ensures that the discussion is based on the organization's identified goals and objectives. Inclusion of these board of education goals makes the rest of the strategy incontrovertible—meaning, there can be no objection—at least at this strategic phase. By leveraging known goals and initiatives, the planner

# Design and Implementation

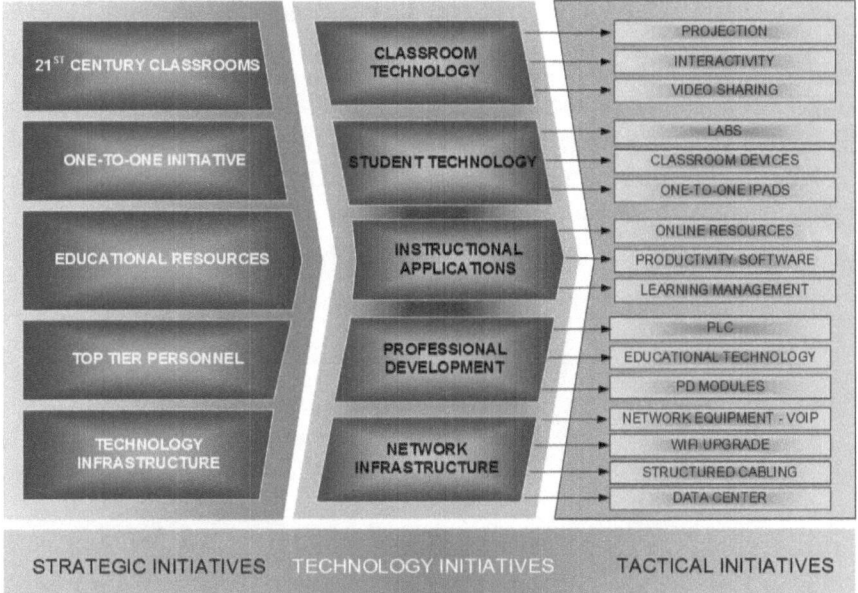

Figure 5.3 Strategic Plan.

grounds the strategy in fundamentals already acknowledged by the district administration.

In this example, the first three Strategic Initiatives, twenty-first-century classrooms, one-to-one, and educational resources were quoted from the district's board of education goals and objectives. The last two, Top Tier Personnel and Technology Infrastructure were quoted from their Local Control and Accountability Plan (LCAP) and a previous Ed Tech Strategic Plan.

Moving from the left to the center column, the plan details the Technology Initiatives that result directly or indirectly in support of the Strategic Initiatives. In other words, the strategic goals drive the technology needs. Therefore, the strategies of the twenty-first-century classroom, and so on, drive the need for, Classroom Technology, Student Technology, Instructional Applications (Education Resources), Professional Development, and Infrastructure (these two should always be there).

The Technology Initiatives then directly drive the need for Tactical Implementation Plans. These initiatives become individual projects, procurements, and deliverables.

By providing this logical progression from strategies based on stated goals and objectives, supported by technology, the planner presents a well-grounded plan for implementation success that all stakeholders should be able to endorse and advocate.

72                     *Chapter Five*

The diagram becomes the tool, brand, or even logo for the strategic plan. The diagram need not be colorful or overly artistic, it simply needs to relate ideas in a well understood and logical progression from strategy to implementation. The modules detailed in the Tactical Initiatives become the projects in the Implementation plan. The fewer words, the better.

Figure 5.4 is a much simpler version of a similar Strategic Technology Plan. In this diagram, the Technology Initiatives lead to Implementation plans.

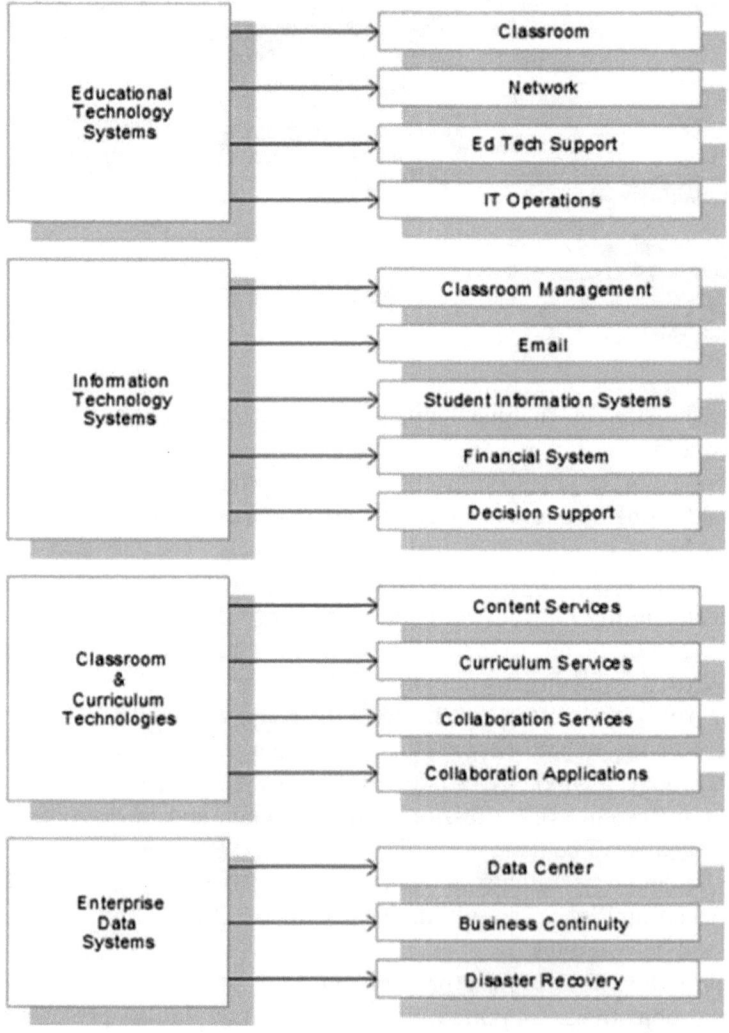

**Figure 5.4  Strategic Plan B.**

It is duly noted that the strategic plan could be a stopping point in a consulting engagement. But the strategic plan and its associated initiatives and budgets are nothing without Tactical Implementation Plans. Each initiative must be assigned management and resources, and undertaken, in a sequence, in order to deliver anything beyond a pile of paper and electronic files.

The strategic plan and the associated logical diagrams become a tool for communicating the strategy and tactics (implementation). The process should always include a formal presentation of this newly documented Technology Strategy to the whole organization or at least to leadership.

This is a true test of the school-leadership's will and acknowledgment of the plan. If the leadership is truly advocating and endorsing the strategy, then communication of the strategy, by leadership becomes the collective call to action to the rest of the school district staff.

A formal presentation to the board of education will cement the organization's commitment to the strategy. If leadership is not willing or able to facilitate this communication, it likely means that this strategic plan will die a quiet death—with few others to worry about its outcomes. Once again, the need for constant communication with several key stakeholders will help mitigate this type of dismal end to a noble endeavor.

When the superintendent employs this type of tool and communicates unequivocal support for its tenets, then each VP, Director, and Principal will be empowered to align himself behind these initiatives. And if the process truly involved each stakeholder at each phase of the development, they should have a fairly intimate understanding of the tenets—even if they don't necessarily agree with them.

Nothing could be more detrimental to a plan than if the rank and file staff don't have any connection to, or understanding of the process used to develop the strategy and the initiatives identified. Once again, involving all possible staff and stakeholders, and keeping them informed of the development of the strategy and definition of the initiatives at each and every milestone, will be the key to successful plan development and communication.

It is for this purpose and reason, the project cannot stop at the delivery of the Education Technology Strategy. The school must commit to developing the Tactical (Implementation) Plans from the very beginning. It must be included in the initial proposal.

The initial phases of the process help identify the strategy. The strategy guides and directs the Technology Initiatives. The Technology Initiatives provide guidance for the Tactical Implementation Plans. The implementation plans provide the technical details to procure and acquire the systems. All according to a prioritization and phasing developed from the feasibility study.

The Strategy is required to ensure the Tactical (Implementation) Plans are aligned and prioritized, but the Strategy by itself delivers nothing but the ability to develop the subordinate implementation plans.

All these components culminate in the Education Technology Strategic Plan Report which delivers the strategy but also each individual plan. So what makes up these plans?

For smaller Education Technology projects, this compiled and printed report including diagrams, spreadsheets, and GANTT charts will easily exceed fifty pages. Cost models, and their details and assumptions will likely take up ten to twenty pages of details in the Appendix of the report. Studies and related white papers may also be included for additional justification and or technical detail. Larger complex plans will go from 200 to 400 pages all told.

Within the Implementation phase is the Tactical Implementation Plan. This is the near-term plan (2–6 months), and should be detailed enough with fully identified funds to begin implementation upon acceptance of the plan.

## SYSTEM DESIGN

The system design diagram is likely the finalized, "proposed" technology architecture developed in the Needs Analysis phase. Recall, in the first section of the Needs Analysis phase a GAP analysis was performed. The outputs of which were the Current Technology Architecture and the Proposed Technology Architecture.

In the Recommendations phase, the drawing was revised again to include the actual technologies, systems, and manufacturers that came to be a part of the final Systems Design. So once again, the planner will revise the recommended technical architecture to a final version that depicts as much detail as is relevant to justify the strategy and tactical plans and satisfy the opinions and concerns of the audience of the report and formal presentation.

Meaning, don't try to cram too much information into a System Design. The purpose of these logical diagrams is to provide a visual abstraction from the technical details—a visual executive overview.

The point being, the FINAL System Design becomes a tool for the reader (think board member or director) to gain a fundamental understanding of the solutions and technologies, but not a complete technical report.

### Planner Perspective

Again, a sideline discussion about the level of technical detail required for strategic plans and Tactical plans. If the strategic plan is a highly technical project, such as a district-wide redundant network, then the technical details will be relevant, especially if a comparison of alternative technologies is part of the Needs Analysis. However, for the most part, leadership level strategic plans should be Educational Goal oriented with a smattering of technology discussion. The best Educational plans only discuss the use of technology to achieve academic goals.

## LOGICAL DESIGN(S)

Depending on the complexity of the overall project(s) there may be one or several logical designs. Alternately, each of these systems may warrant their own logical design within its own project plan and budget. For instance, in the Scenario Two—Student Information System (SIS) Selection, the Proposed Hardware Logical Design might depict the implementation of Wi-Fi systems along with Backup and Disaster Recovery systems all installed within a new data center. While the Proposed SIS Logical Design would depict the server/OS platforms within the data center compute platform.

This becomes a matter of focus and granularity that the planner must determine. Keeping in mind that the purpose of the plan is not to detail every data point to the Nth degree, but to provide enough data to the key stakeholders in order to provide justification to expend funding. That's it. If the project can get the funding with a cloud diagram scratched on a napkin over lunch, then a lot of this formality (especially the up-front processes) could be abridged in order to get right into implementation.

That is not to suggest that the implementation plans could be developed any other way, but the formality may not be as rigid if the funding is readily available and the stakeholders and leadership are ready to spend the money. That's why the word abridged was used instead of obviated. The planning process may be shortened and less formalized, but the necessary research and compilation must still be performed in order to maintain the integrity and credibility of decision making and recommendation processes. And, getting approval for a set of initiatives totaling over a million dollars, typically will need a lot of backup and justification.

In school districts in California, any expenditure in excess of $50,000 typically warrants approval by the board of education and the supporting documentation must be clear and concise.

Logical designs are intended to depict technology systems in a most fundamental manner to allow nontechnical stakeholders to gain an understanding of how the technologies fit with each other and within the organization. Meaning that the planner must determine the appropriate scope of the logical diagram.

It is all too often that a network or systems engineer is asked to provide a drawing that would be virtually useless for the strategic plan. The planner cannot rely on the technical staff to provide drawings or diagrams of the nature required for the CEO or the school board member without significant modification. And what typically happens, since the engineers are typically not graphic artists, the planner must engage with a more graphics-oriented type diagram that includes less technical detail but engenders more of a "this fits here, and this goes there" type of delivery—basically starting from scratch.

If the technology system calls for a new wide-area network (WAN) architecture, then the logical design should depict the locations, telecommunication services (bandwidth), and likely some boxes that depict the equipment that must be purchased in the typical hierarchical or hub and spoke topology.

This type of diagram communicates the connectivity between locations. The focus on topology allows the executives and leadership to understand that this equipment and services will connect the remote sites together. It would not be beneficial for the executives and leadership to know the routing protocols or the IP mapping—things the network engineer would typically include in his drawing. The drawings need not be to scale, reflect actual geographic maps, or include IP addresses or subnet maps.

However, in a dark fiber cost analysis, geographic mapping of distances and pathways would be the focus. Applications or computing resources at the various locations would not be relevant.

Alternately, for the SIS Selection project, the logical design should depict the compute and storage platforms within the data center. The compute platforms are typically segregated by hardware platforms as well as operating systems. Although the executives and leadership don't need to know the licensing or configuration details of the operating systems, it is helpful for them to understand the relationships between hardware, operating systems, applications, and oftentimes, backup and archival systems within the diagrams will settle fears of catastrophic system failures and mitigate questions not relevant to the scope.

## DESIGN NARRATIVE

(Deja Vu coming) So if a picture is worth a thousand words, the Design Narrative are those thousand words. Unfortunately, those logical design representations drawn so logically, communicate little without some accompaniment. Whether through a verbal description or through written text, the design narrative fills in the blanks of the logical diagrams. And once again, not focusing on the technical details that the network engineer needs, but to describe in verbiage the relationship between components, and the proverbial—what and why?

Once again, these components of the final report can be exhaustive or vague. It will be contingent on the planner to determine the level of granularity, technical detail, and specificity based on the size, complexity, and political (fiscal) environment. To reiterate, if the projects can get funded by a simple PowerPoint slide and budget spreadsheet, so be it. But rest assured, if the school district is fiscally responsible, looking at cost effectivity, and under any audit or scrutiny, the granular details better be there. All the way down to manufacturer's warranties, shipping, and taxes.

One of the reasons it's called a design "narrative" is because this section of the report(s) should be written as prose in sentence and paragraph format. It should not be a technical training or primer. It is intended to bring lay-persons into the realm of technology without requiring an IT certification.

In fact, the effort is to communicate the need and benefit, without the agony of technical comparison and option analysis. Anything technical in this type of report will never be read and will detract from the overall report. The planner should leave the technical details, dimensions, system configurations, software versions, and compatibility listing to the Appendix of the report as supporting documentation if he needs another 100 pages to make the binder another 4 pounds heavier.

### Planner Perspectives

Too often, technical staff utilize bulleted lists to provide information and reporting. This format is not appropriate for the Design Narrative. Although a bulleted list might be a part of the overall report to list a set of features/functions, the design narrative should provide the reader a stream of consciousness description which moves them through the accompanying diagrams to form a complete understanding of the project or initiative.

The design narrative is also the planner's opportunity to highlight important design points and technologies as they support the plan.

## PHYSICAL LAYOUTS

Physical layouts are typically site plans or floor plans limited in detail to the scope of the project. Once again, it becomes very important to provide enough information for the decision-makers and stakeholders. It isn't appropriate to provide them with construction documents and design specifications, although these might be part of the procurement requirements when time comes to implement. They also don't need to know the fire escape routes (oftentimes the only existing floor plans available are the fire escape routes—these diagrams are rarely to scale and are usually missing minor walls, hallways, and building entrances/exits. For technology strategic or implementation plan applications, these types of floor plans are better left out of the report).

Scaled drawings, maps, and floor plans are more typically required for projects that include construction and engineering. For instance, if a new data center is being built on an existing plot of land, the implementation plan may require the scaled drawing, but not each architectural and trade drawing.

If part of the project is to show some internal tenant improvements in an existing building, the simple floor plan that shows what will go where is appropriate.

Physical layouts for structured cabling projects may be required for bidding and estimation, but not for a strategic planning report.

However, if the strategic plan calls for a $20 million data center, there better be an artist's 3D computer walk-through and scale model to justify the expenditure.

## IMPLEMENTATION PLAN(S) AND TIMELINE (GANTT CHART)

The next most significant document after the System Design plan is the project timeline, typically represented using the GANTT chart. GANTT charts are widely known and understood, and can easily be generated using Microsoft Project or another project management tool.

One important consideration when generating GANTT charts for an implementation plan is that the elapsed time will not directly correlate to resource scheduling. For instance, when scheduling a resource for network engineering, that resource would be required during the assessment and planning process, but not for the several weeks between the planning and the actual implementation. If he was kept on staff during this dead period, the resource staffing estimates may be thrown off. Once again, all documents and diagrams provided as part of the strategic plan need only be detailed enough for executive-level approvals.

However, once the planner gets into implementation planning and ROM estimates for the implementation plan, these details will become more detailed and important.

If the GANTT chart is used for project planning, the planner may decide to actually use a different tool for actual project management. This issue will be discussed in depth in the MAPIT™ Project Management book (Technology Planning for your School—MAPIT™ Project Management).

Typically the most important information that is communicated via the GANTT chart is the start date, end date, and the phasing of the projects. Different departments and resources can visually identify where their roles and responsibilities come into the plan.

Use a high-level GANTT chart for the strategic plan, and then the more detailed task level GANTT charts for the individual implementation plans. MS Project provides ultimate flexibility to enter, view, and save timelines in many different ways to best support efforts to show a well thought-out strategy and tactical plan.

Just as the design narrative accompanies and provides detailed clarity to the logical design diagrams, the implementation plan should communicate sequence and duration detail for each individual plan.

Consider that each individual project is a chapter in a book correlating to the timeline. The information in each chapter once again in relevant detail to the target audience, addressing who, what, when, and how (the why should have been answered long ago). But this is where the planner must also recognize how each individual project will require these details and begin to lay the ground-work for these project details.

## ROM BUDGET ESTIMATES—COST MODEL

The planner can always tell who's in the money when he gets to this part of the formal presentation. The CEO and the CFO (CBO) will start to look at these numbers real hard. It really is the moment of truth. Take heed, no one better be surprised by the numbers presented in the cost model because throughout the process (Recommendations and Feasibility) the planner should have had numerous discussions about the initial cost estimates and the available funding.

Also, recall that the feasibility study requires a meeting with the person who knows about the money—this is NOT the IT director, he only knows about his money.

The cost estimates presented in the Final report should be ROM3 or higher. Typically, the ROM is reviewed and revised many times by the planner and his internal team before the report is published and presented. The more time that lapses from report completion to publication will likely require the ROM to be continually revised until the publication of the report.

## FINAL NOTES

These aren't really the final notes. As stated repeatedly, developing a plan just produces a bunch of paper and electronic files. Their value is in their research, logic, solution sets, budgets, and plans. These planning outputs become the Project Management inputs, which means—take the plans, and go directly to MAPIT™ Project Management—which is the next book! See you in Implementation!

## CHAPTER FIVE ESSENTIALS

1. Although the strategic plan and associated diagrams are key deliverables of the planning process, they are only milestones. A strategic plan without its component implementation plans is just a list of talking points. The implementation plans are the deliverables that a project manager can act on.
2. The Education Technology Strategic Plan is the compilation of all the deliverables starting in Needs Identification and through each of the phases.
3. The communication of this strategy should be formal and delivered to all stakeholders with the endorsement of the superintendent.
4. The ROM cost model should be all encompassing and fully funded through the initial phases.
5. The planner should be prepared to discuss the implementation plans and timelines in order to move directly into implementation.

# About the Author

**Darryl Vidal** has been involved with technology and education all his adult life. Starting in aerospace telecommunications, he worked as a systems engineer for Apple Computer in the late 1980s and began working directly with K–12 schools. By 1994, Darryl began providing technology consulting services to San Diego Unified School District and many other districts in the region, helping design and implement digital classrooms, wide area networks, VoIP, and wireless campuses.

For over twenty years, Darryl has been working on the forefront of Education Technology modernization programs from Virtual Classroom Technology, through Learning Management Systems, helping plan and manage school technology upgrades totaling over $500,000,000.00.

Books by Darryl Vidal—published by Rowman & Littlefield Education

*Next Practices: An Executive Guide for Education Decision Makers*
*Vision: The First Critical Step in Developing a Strategy for Educational Technology*
*Confucius in the Technology Realm: A Philosophical Approach to Your School's Ed Tech Goals*

www.ingramcontent.com/pod-product-compliance
Lightning Source LLC
Chambersburg PA
CBHW030148240426
43672CB00005B/314